junie b. jones®
Loves
Handsome Warren

by BARBARA PARK

illustrated by
Denise Brunkus

Junie B. Jones Loves Handsome Warren by Barbara Park

Text copyright © 1996 by Barbara Park
Cover art and interior illustrations copyright © 1996 by Denise Brunkus
All rights reserved.

This bilingual edition was published by Longtail Books in 2022 by arrangement with Barbara Park c/o Writers House LLC through KCC(Korea Copyright Center Inc.), Seoul.

No part of this publication may be reproduced, stored in a retrieval system, or transmitted, in any form or by any means, graphic, electronic, or mechanical, including photocopying, taping, and recording, without prior written permission from the publisher.
For information about permission, write to editor@longtailbooks.co.kr

ISBN 979-11-91343-14-4 14740

Longtail, Inc.

Contents

1

Handsome Warren

My name is Junie B. Jones. The B **stand**s
for Beatrice. **Except** I don't like Beatrice.

I just like B and **that's all**.

I am in the **grade** of **kindergarten**.

My room is named Room Nine.

I have two bestest[1] friends at that place.

One of them is named Lucille.

---

1 **bestest** 단어 'best(최고의)'를 강조한 비격식적인 표현. '최고로 좋은'
이라는 뜻을 나타내며 어린아이가 주로 사용한다.

She is way beautifuller[2] than me. That's because her **nanna** buys her **fancy** dresses. Plus also she has **lacy** socks with ribbons on them.

My other friend is named Grace. Me and that Grace **ride** the school bus together.

She has my favorite kind of hair. It is called *automatically curly*.

Also, she has pink high tops.[3] And fast feet.

That Grace is the fastest runner in all of kindergarten.

She wins me at all of our **race**s.

I am a good **sport** about it. Except for

---

2 **beautifuller** 형용사 'beautiful'의 비교급을 잘못 만든 것으로, 올바른 표현은 'more beautiful'이다.

3 **high top** 하이 톱. 발목 부분이 길어 복사뼈까지 덮는 형태로 된 운동화.

sometimes I call her the name of *cheater pants.*

Me and that Grace and Lucille play horses together before school.

Horses is when you **gallop**. And **trot**. And **snort**.

I am Brownie. Lucille is Blackie. And that Grace is Yellowie.

Only today, me and that Grace couldn't find Lucille anywhere.

We looked all over the place for her.

"Darn it,[4]" I said. "Now we can't play horses that good. 'Cause two horses isn't as fun as three horses."

"Maybe she's just late," said that Grace.

---

4 **darn it** 'damn it(빌어먹을)'을 순화한 것으로, 못마땅하거나 짜증스러울 때 쓰는 속어적 표현.

"Or else maybe something went wrong at her house."

I **tap**ped on my **chin** very thinking.

"Yes," I said. "Maybe her grampa[5] brought a **parrot** to her house. And Lucille was getting dressed for school. And then the parrot flew into her room. And he got all **tangle**d up in her hair. And so her grampa had to call 911. And a **real live** fireman came to her house. And he cut the parrot out of her hair with scissors. Only that left a **teeny bald**y[6] **spot**. But guess what? If you wear a big **bow**, nobody can

---

5 **grampa** '할아버지(grandpa)'를 부르는 말로, 'gramp', 'grampa', 'grampy' 등 다양한 표현이 있다.

6 **baldy** '머리가 벗겨진'이라는 뜻의 단어 'bald'를 주니 B.가 'baldy' 라고 장난스럽게 말한 표현. 이 책에 나오는 'jazzy up' 또한 이와 같은 경우이다.

even tell the difference."

That Grace looked **curious** at my big bow.

I did a **gulp**.

"Yeah, only **pretend** I didn't even tell you that," I said very soft.

After that, me and that Grace looked for Lucille some more.

And guess what?

I spotted her! That's what!

"HEY, GRACE! I SEE HER! I SEE LUCILLE! SHE IS RUNNING PAST THE **WATER FOUNTAIN**!"

That Grace spotted her, too.

"HEY! SOMEBODY'S **CHASING** HER, JUNIE B.!" she **yell**ed. "WHO *IS* THAT BOY? WHO IS THAT BOY WHO IS

CHASING LUCILLE?"

I **squint**ed my eyes very harder.

"IT IS AN **EVIL** *STRANGER BOY,*
GRACE!" I shouted back. "AN EVIL
STRANGER BOY IS CHASING LUCILLE!
AND SO NOW YOU AND ME WILL
HAVE TO SAVE HER!"

I **wave**d my arm in a fast circle.

"Come on, Yellowie! Let's go! Let's go save Lucille!"

Then me and that Grace **spring**ed[7] into action!

We galloped our fastest after the

---

7 **springed** (sprang) 영어권 국가의 아이들이 동사의 과거형을 말할 때 모든 단어의 끝에 '-ed'를 붙이는 실수를 종종 한다. 이 책에 나오는 'runned(ran)', 'hided(hid)' 등이 이와 같은 경우이다.

stranger!

That Grace **caught up** to him **speedy** quick.

She **shoo**ed her arms all around.

"GO AWAY, BOY! GO AWAY AND LEAVE LUCILLE ALONE!" she shouted.

"YES!" I yelled. "LEAVE LUCILLE ALONE! OR I WILL **TELL PRINCIPAL ON** YOU! 'CAUSE ME AND HIM ARE **PERSONAL** FRIENDS. AND HE WILL **POUND** YOUR HEAD!"

After that, me and that Grace kept on shooing our arms until he ran away.

Then we did a **high five**.

"**HURRAY**!" we shouted. "HURRAY! HURRAY! WE SAVED LUCILLE FROM THE EVIL STRANGER BOY!"

All of a sudden, Lucille came **stomp**ing at us very angry.

"WHY DID YOU DO THAT?" she **holler**ed. "WHY DID YOU CHASE THAT BOY AWAY? NOW YOU'VE **RUIN**ED *EVERYTHING!*"

Me and that Grace looked surprised at her.

"But we thought you *wanted* us to do that," said that Grace.

"We saved you from the evil stranger boy," I explained very **proud**.

Lucille did a mad breath.

"He is *not* an evil stranger boy, Junie B.! He's a new kid in Room Eight. And his name is Warren! And he's the handsomest boy I ever saw! He's even been in a *TV*

commercial before!"

Me and that Grace raised up our **eyebrow**s.

"He has?" said that Grace.

"He's been in a TV commercial before?" I said.

That Grace stood on her **tip**py-**toe**s.

"Where did he go? I didn't even get a good look at him," she said.

"Me too," I said. "I didn't get a good look at him, too. How handsome is he, Lucille? Is he handsome like a movie star?"

Just then, that Grace jumped up and down very excited.

"THERE HE IS! THERE HE IS! HE'S OVER THERE UNDER THAT TREE! SEE HIM, JUNIE B.? SEE HIM?"

I squinted my hardest at that guy.

Then my eyes **practically pop**ped out of my head!

'Cause he *was* handsome like a movie star! That's why!

"Wowie-wow-wow! What a *chunk!*" I said. "I would like him for my new boyfriend, I think!"

Lucille made angry eyes at me.

"No!" she hollered. "Don't say that, Junie B.! He can't be *your* boyfriend. He can only be *my* boyfriend. 'Cause I saw him first!"

I **thought** it **over** very **careful**.

"Yeah, only here's the problem, Lucille," I said. "Me and Grace didn't actually get a **crack** at him yet."

"Yeah," said that Grace. "We **definite**ly need a crack at him. And so now you have to introduce us."

Lucille **stamp**ed her foot.

"No!" she yelled. "No! No! No! 'Cause you guys will **steal** him away from me! And that's not even **fair**! Plus, Junie B. already *has* a boyfriend. Remember, Junie B.? You already have Ricardo! Remember?"

I did another **peek** at Handsome Warren.

"Yeah, only I think I may be ready to **move on**," I said very quiet.

That's when Lucille's face got **boiling mad**. And she stomped away from us speedy quick.

Only me and that Grace didn't even

care.

We just kept peeking and peeking at that handsome boy.

'Cause he was beauty to our eyes.

2
Pigs[1]

Lucille sits next to me in Room Nine.

I kept on being nice to her.

'Cause I wanted to meet that handsome boy, of course.

"Want to be friends again, Lucille? Huh? Want to be friends like we used to be? That would be nice of us, don't you

---

1 pig '돼지'라는 원래의 뜻 말고 여기에서 사용된 것처럼 불쾌하거나 무례한 사람을 가리키는 표현으로도 쓰인다.

think?"

"No," said Lucille. "You only want to be friends so you can **steal** my new boyfriend."

I did a big breath at her.

"Yeah, only how can I even steal him, Lucille?" I asked. "'Cause you are way beautifuller than me. Remember that? Remember how beautifuller than me you are?"

Lucille remembered.

She **fluff**ed herself.

Then she showed me her new **lacy** socks.

"Eight dollars and fifty cents . . . *not* **including tax**," she said.

I **bug**ged **out** my eyes at them.

"Wowie-wow-wow. Those are some **fancy** feet you have there, madam!" I said.

After that, I showed Lucille *my* socks, too.

"See, Lucille? See mine? They are very **sag**ging and **droopy**. That's because last night me and my dog Tickle played **tug**-of-war[2] with those things. And he got

drooly on them."

Lucille **made a face**.

"Eew," she said.

"I know they are eew," I said back. "That's what I've been trying to tell you, Lucille. I am a big pig. And so how can I even steal your boyfriend?"

Just then, Lucille looked nicer at me.

I **scoot**ed my chair close to her.

"Now we are friends again! Right, Lucille? Right?" I said. "And so now you can introduce me to Handsome Warren. 'Cause I won't even steal that guy."

Lucille fluffed herself some more.

"I don't know . . . I'll think about it," she

---

2 **tug-of-war** 줄다리기. 여러 사람이 편을 갈라, 굵은 밧줄을 마주 잡고 당겨서 승부를 겨루는 놀이.

said.

I **clap**ped my hands real **thrill**ed.

Then I quick stood up on my chair.

"GRACE! HEY, GRACE!" I **holler**ed.

"LUCILLE SAID SHE'LL THINK ABOUT
IT!"

Just then, I heard a different voice.

"JUNIE B. JONES! WHAT DO YOU
THINK YOU ARE DOING?"

It was my teacher.

Her name is Mrs.

She has another name, too. But I just

like Mrs. and **that's all**.

I smiled kind of nervous.

"I am trying to get a message to Grace," I said very soft.

Mrs. hurried up to my table.

"Never *ever* stand up in your chair, Junie B.," she said. "You could fall off and break something."

"Yeah!" shouted a **meanie** boy named Jim. "She could break the *floor* with her hard *head!*"

I made a **fist** at that kid.

"PLUS ALSO I COULD BREAK YOUR WHOLE **ENTIRE** BEAN BRAIN![3]" I hollered back.

---

3 **bean brain** '바보' 또는 '멍청이'라는 뜻의 속어.

Mrs. **plop**ped me back in my seat.

"That's enough," she **grouch**ed. "I **mean** it, Junie B. Not one more word."

After that, I stayed in my chair very good. And I did my work.

I did my **spell**ing.

And my **arithmetic**.

And my **print**ing.

Also, I drew a sausage patty[4] on my arm.

Only that wasn't even an **assignment**.

That is called *working on your own*.

Pretty soon, Mrs. clapped her loud hands together.

---

4 **patty** 패티. 쇠고기, 돼지고기, 생선 등을 다져 빵가루, 소금, 후추 등을 넣고 동글납작하게 반죽한 다음 구워 먹는 요리.

"Okay, everyone. It's almost time for **recess**. Pass in your papers and line up at the door."

Mrs. looked at me.

"And please . . . let's be ladies and gentlemen about it."

Ladies and gentlemen means No **Trampling** Thy[5] **Neighbor**.

It is a Ten Commandments,[6] I think.

Me and Lucille held hands.

"Now you're gonna introduce me. Right, Lucille? Now I'm gonna get to meet that handsome boy."

Just then, that Grace runned up behind

---

5 **thy** 2인칭 소유격 대명사 'your(너의)'의 고어.

6 **Ten Commandments** 십계명. 기독교에서 하나님이 시나이산에서 모세를 통하여 이스라엘 백성에게 내렸다고 하는 열 가지 계율.

us.

I was happy to see her.

"Grace! Grace! Guess what? Lucille is going to introduce us to Handsome Warren! 'Cause you and me are big pigs, that's why!"

That Grace looked **upset** at me.

"I am *not* a big pig," she said.

I quick **whisper**ed in her ear. "Yeah, only we're not *really* big pigs, Grace. We just have to *say* we're big pigs. Or else Lucille thinks we will steal her boyfriend. Get it?"

That Grace got it.

"I am a **giant stink hog**," she said to Lucille.

And so after that, all of us **skip**ped to

the **swing** set very happy.

We sat down. And waited for Room Eight to come out.

We waited a real long time.

Then **all of a sudden**, Room Eight opened their door! And Handsome Warren came out of there!

Lucille runned to him and **grab**bed his hand.

She pulled him to the swings to meet us.

"*That* is Grace. And *that* is Junie B. Jones," she said to Handsome Warren.

He **wave**d very cute and **friendly**.

I quick hided behind my hands.

'Cause all of a sudden I felt **shy** of that guy.

I **peek**ed through my fingers.

"Peekaboo.[7] I see you," I said.

Then I laughed and laughed. 'Cause I'm a laugh a minute,[8] that's why.

I kept on laughing at that funny **joke**.

Only too bad for me.

'Cause after while, I couldn't even stop.

I was out of **control**, I think.

I holded my **side**s and fell on the ground.

Then I **roll**ed and laughed and rolled and laughed. All around in the grass.

Handsome Warren looked nervous of me.

He backed up.

---

7 **peekaboo** 까꿍. 어린아이를 어를 때 내는 소리로, 주로 손으로 얼굴을 가렸다가 갑자기 얼굴을 보여 주는 놀이를 할 때 사용하는 말이다.

8 **a laugh a minute** '아주 웃기는 사람' 또는 '아주 재미있는 것'이라는 뜻의 속어.

"What a nutball,[9]" he said very soft.

Then he turned around. And walked away.

And Lucille and that Grace walked with him.

---

9 **nutball** '괴짜', '미치광이'라는 뜻의 속어.

3
Not a Nutball

Mrs. **blew** her **whistle**.

That means *come in from recess*.

Lucille and that Grace ran to get me.

'Cause I was still in the grass, that's why.

Lucille was happy and **sparkly**.

"Didn't you *love* him, Junie B.? Wasn't
he so handsome? He was even handsomer
up close, don't you think? He was nice,
too. Wasn't he nice?"

That Grace was happy and sparkly, too.

"He said he liked my high tops," she told me.

"He said he liked my dress," said Lucille.

"He said I was a nutball," I said.

Lucille **twirl**ed all around.

"Not me," she said. "He didn't say *I* was a nutball. That's because he loves me!"

That Grace jumped high in the air.

"Me too! He loves me, too!" she said real **squeal**y.[1]

Just then, Lucille stopped twirling.

She **cross**ed **her arms**.

"No, Grace," she said. "He does *not* love

---

1 **squealy** 주니 B.가 만들어 낸 말로 단어 'squeal(꽥 소리를 내다)'의 뒤에 '-y'를 붙여 '꽥꽥거리며'라는 의미의 부사로 사용하였다.

you, too. He only loves me. 'Cause I saw him first. And you're not allowed to **steal** him away, remember?"

That Grace crossed *her* arms, too.

"I'm not *stealing* him away, Lucille. He just **automatic**ally loves me on his own. And there's nothing I can do about it," she said.

I **tug**ged on Lucille's dress.

"How come he said I was a nutball, do you think? Why did he have to say that **dumb** thing?"

Lucille didn't pay **attention** to me. She kept on being mad at that Grace.

"I knew it!" she **grouch**ed. "I knew this was going to happen, Grace! You're trying to steal my boyfriend! Junie B. said you wouldn't! But you are!"

She looked down at me.

"Tell her, Junie B.! Tell Grace she can't steal my boyfriend!"

I looked **curious** at her.

"I am not a nutball. Am I? Am I a nutball?" I said. "I am not a nutball."

Just then, that Grace **lean**ed close to Lucille's nose.

"I CAN LOVE ANYBODY I WANT TO, LUCILLE!" she hollered in her face.

"NO, YOU CAN*NOT*, GRACE!"

"YES, I CAN, *TOO*, LUCILLE!"

I **tap**ped on both their **ankle**s.

"How many think I'm a nutball? Raise your hand," I said.

Just then, Mrs. blew her whistle again.

And so I stood up from the grass. And I walked to Room Nine all **by myself**.

'Cause I couldn't stop thinking about being a nutball, that's why.

I thought about it the whole rest of the

day.

I didn't even talk.

Not at Show-and-Tell.[2]

Not at **snack**time.

Not even when I got on the bus to **ride** home.

That Grace sat down next to me. She was happy and sparkly again.

"I *know* he loves me better than Lucille," she said. "I'm **positive** he does. And he hasn't even seen how fast I can run yet."

She **poke**d me with her finger.

"Who do you think he likes better? Me or Lucille? And tell the truth," she said.

---

2 **show-and-tell** 유치원이나 초등학교에서 주로 하는 수업 활동의 하나로, 학생들이 각자 자신에게 의미 있는 물건을 가지고 와서 그것에 대해 발표하는 시간이다.

I still didn't talk.

That Grace **jiggle**d me.

"How come you're not talking, Junie B.?" she asked. "How come you're not answering me? Are you sick? Do you have a **sore throat**?"

Just then, her eyes opened real wide. And her whole mouth came open.

"Ohhhhh . . . I know why you're not talking. It's because you're **upset**, right? You're upset that you're a nutball."

I **spin**ned around at her very quick.

"I am *not* a nutball, Grace! I am just a **regular** normal girl. And I don't even know why that boy had to call me that!"

"*I* do," said that Grace. "I know why he called you that. It's because you couldn't stop laughing. And you fell in the grass. And you **roll**ed all around down there."

I **stare**d at her.

"Yeah? So?" I said.

"So that's how nutballs act," said that Grace. "And I should know. 'Cause I have a nutball right in my own **personal** family."

I raised up my **eyebrow**s.

"You do?" I said.

"Yes," she said. "My two-year-old brother Jeffie is a nutball. Every time we go to the mall, we have to put him on a **leash**. Or else he **tackle**s people. And then he hides in the clothes and **Security** has to come."

She looked at me very **suspicious**.

"Did *you* ever do that, Junie B. Jones?

Hmmm? Did *you* ever tackle people? And hide in the clothes and Security had to come?"

I quick looked away from her.

'Cause that is my own personal beeswax.[3]

"Jeffie's not allowed to eat sugar cereal anymore, either," said that Grace. "My mother thinks the sugar gets him all **jazz**ied **up**."

She raised one eyebrow very curious.

"Do *you* eat sugar cereal for breakfast, Junie B.? Hmmm? *Do* you?" she asked.

I looked away again.

---

3 **beeswax** '일' 또는 '용무'라는 뜻으로 'mind your own business(당신의 일에나 신경 쓰세요)'와 같은 표현에서 발음이 유사한 business를 좀 더 부드럽게 말할 때 사용한다.

'Cause guess what?

More of my own personal beeswax.

That's what.

4
Fibers[1]

It was the next morning.

I gave Tickle my sugar cereal.

I gave him my Sweetie Puffs.[2] And my

Crackle Berries.[3] And my Happy Smacky

---

1 **fiber** 섬유질. 주로 식물에 함유된 실 모양 물질로, 그중 인간이 섭취할 수 있는 것을 식이 섬유라고 한다. 콜레스테롤 조절 및 변비 예방에 효과가 있다.

2 **Sweetie Puffs** 가상의 시리얼. 'Puffs'라는 이름에서 동그란 구체 모양을 한 시리얼이라는 것을 알 수 있다.

3 **Crackle Berries** 가상의 시리얼. 'Berries'라는 이름에서 블루베리나 크랜베리와 같은 딸기류의 맛이 나는 시리얼이라는 것을 알 수 있다.

Flakes.[4]

He loved eating that **stuff** very much.

Then he runned in the living room. And

---

4 **Happy Smacky Flakes** 가상의 시리얼. 'Flakes'라는 이름에서 옥
  수숫가루에 소금, 설탕, 꿀 등을 넣어 얇게 가공하여 만든 콘플레이크
  (cornflakes)류의 시리얼이라는 것을 알 수 있다.

.

he **throw**ed **up** on the **rug**.

Mother **scream**ed real loud.

That's how come I hided under the **sink**. But she and Daddy found me there.

They did not **handle** theirselves that **professional**.

"WHY, JUNIE B.? WHY WOULD YOU DO SUCH A THING!" shouted Daddy very loud.

"DO WE HAVE TO WATCH YOU EVERY MINUTE?" shouted Mother very loud.

Just then, my grandma Helen Miller walked in the front door.

"Grandma Miller! Grandma Miller! I love you! I love you!" I shouted.

Then I runned to her **speedy** fast. And

I hided in her coat till Mother and Daddy left for work.

After that, my grandma let me pick a new cereal to eat.

I picked a **grown-up** kind.

It was the kind with fibers in it.

"This kind is good for me. Right, Grandma? This kind won't even **jazz**y me **up**."

Then I put that delicious stuff in my mouth.

And I **chew**ed and chewed. Only it didn't actually **grind** up that good.

I chewed on it the whole **entire** morning.

I was still chewing when that Grace got on my school bus.

She ran to me very excited.

"Look, Junie B.! Look what my mother bought me!" she said.

She holded up her foot.

"New running shoes!" she said. "See them? See the **lightning stripe**s on the sides! That means I can run as fast as lightning! And so now Warren will love me the best for sure!"

I pointed at my mouth.

"Yeah, only I can't actually **discuss** this right now, Grace. 'Cause I'm chewing fibers here," I said.

I opened up to show her.

"See them in there? They are **stuck** in my teeth, I think."

After that, I **poke**d all around with my

fingernail. And I **suck**ed them out.

I **smack**ed my **lip**s together.

"Good news. I think I'm done," I said.

That Grace tried to show me her shoes again.

"Yeah, only sorry, Grace. But I still can't talk yet. 'Cause I have to do something very important."

Then I **lean**ed back in my seat.

And I closed my eyes.

And I didn't move for lots of seconds.

All of a sudden, I **clap**ped my hands very **joyful**.

"Did you *see* me, Grace? Did you see how *calm* I was just then? That's because I don't have sugar in me today! And I can sit **still** very excellent!"

I **hug**ged her real tight.

"It worked, Grace! The fiber cereal worked! Now I'm not a nutball anymore! And so Handsome Warren will love me just like he loves you!"

That Grace did not look happy.

She **bend**ed down and **dust**ed her new shoes.

I bended down there with her.

"How come you're not happy, Grace? How come you're not happy that he will love me, too?" I asked.

She did a **huffy** breath.

"You're **breathing** on the shoes," she said. "Don't breathe on the shoes."

Just then, the bus stopped at school.

I looked out the window and clapped

my hands real **thrill**ed.

"Grace! Grace! I see Handsome Warren! He's at the **water fountain**! And Lucille isn't even there yet!"

All of a sudden that Grace's face got very **perky**.

She **zoom**ed off the bus like a **speed**ing **bullet**. And she ran to Handsome Warren zippity[5] quick.

I could hear her shouting all over the **playground**.

"LOOK, WARREN! LOOK AT MY NEW SHOES!" she **yell**ed. "THEY HAVE LIGHTNING ON THE SIDES! SEE?"

She was running in circles around that

---

5 **zippity** 단어 'zippy(아주 빠른)'를 강조하여 말한 것으로, 'zippity quick'은 '아주 빠르게'라는 뜻의 비격식적 표현이다.

handsome guy.

"Wanna have a **race**?" she asked him. "Wanna see how fast I am? **Bet** you can't **beat** me, Warren! Bet you can't beat me in a race!"

And so just then, Handsome Warren and that Grace raced all over the playground.

And he couldn't even beat her.

He came back very **pooped**.

"Wow," he said. "You're the fastest runner I ever saw. Maybe someday you'll be in the Olympics.[6]"

"I will, Warren!" said that Grace. "I will be in the Olympics someday! Wanna race

---

6 **Olympics** 올림픽. 4년마다 열리는 국제 운동 경기 대회로 1896년 그리스의 아테네에서 제1회 대회가 개최된 이후로 지금까지 이어지고 있다.

me again? Huh? Do you?"

Just then, Lucille **pop**ped in **out of nowhere**.

She had on the beautifullest dress I ever saw.

She **spin**ned all around.

"Ooooo, Lucille. You look like a **royal highness** in that thing," I said.

"I know it," she said. "This is the kind of dress that *princesses* wear. It is made out of rich red velvet.[7]"

She **twirl**ed in front of Handsome Warren.

"This dress costed over one hundred and fifty dollars . . . *not* **including tax**," she said.

All of a sudden, Handsome Warren's eyes got big and wide.

"Wow! You must be the richest girl in the whole school!" he said.

Lucille **fluff**ed her hair.

---

7 **velvet** 벨벳. 짧고 부드러운 솜털이 광택을 내는 고급 원단.

"I am," she said. "I *am* the richest girl in the whole school, Warren. Guess how much my shoes cost? Just guess, okay?"

Just then I jumped right in front of that guy's face.

"Hello. How are you today?" I said very **pleasant**. "I am fine. I am fine and calm."

He backed up from me.

"Yeah, only you don't even have to be afraid," I said. "'Cause I ate fibers for breakfast. And I am so calm I could go to sleep, probably. Want to see me? Huh, Warren? Want to see me go to sleep?"

I **plop**ped down in the grass.

"Look, Warren. See me down here? I am not even laughing and rolling. I am just being calm. And **that's all**."

I put my head on the ground.

"Watch me go to sleep, Warren. Watch
me. Watch me."

I closed my eyes and opened them
again.

"Did you see that, Warren? Huh? Did you see me go to sleep? See? I *told* you I was calm. Didn't I? Huh? Didn't I tell you?"

Handsome Warren looked and looked at

me.

Then he did the cuckoo **sign**.[8]

And he walked away to the **swing**s.

And Lucille and that Grace walked with him.

---

8 **cuckoo sign** '미쳤다'라는 의미로 관자놀이 주변에서 손가락을 빙빙 돌리는 행동을 말한다. 여기에서 cuckoo는 바보나 이상한 사람을 가리키는 속어이다.

5
Hurray for Princess Clothes!

That night at dinner, a great idea came in my head.

It came during my macaroni.[1]

"HEY! I JUST THOUGHT OF IT!" I shouted. "I JUST THOUGHT OF HOW TO GET THAT HANDSOME GUY TO LOVE ME!"

---

1 **macaroni** 마카로니. 길이가 짧고, 튜브 모양을 한 이탈리아식 밀가루 면의 일종.

I **stuff**ed in more macaroni.

"HURRY, EVERYBODY! EAT! EAT! WE
GOTTA GET TO THE MALL BEFORE IT
CLOSES!"

Just then, two macaronis fell out of my
mouth. And onto the floor. And my dog
named Tickle ate them.

Daddy **made a face**.

"Hey, hey, hey! Slow down! What's the
hurry?" he said.

"We gotta get to the mall! That's what's
the hurry! We have to buy me a princess
dress! Plus also I need some shoes with
lightning!"

Mother and Daddy looked funny at me.

That's how come I had to explain all
about Handsome Warren. And how he

loved Lucille's princess dress. And how he loved Grace's fast shoes.

"And so now *I* will get a princess dress! Plus also I will get shoes with lightning! And then Warren will love *me*, too!"

I **wipe**d my mouth with my hand. Then I quick jumped down from my chair.

"'Scuse me, please! 'Scuse me from the table! 'Cause I'm all **fill**ed **up**!"

I runned down the **hall**. And **zoom**ed into the **nursery**.

The nursery is where my baby brother named Ollie lives.

"YOU GUYS DO THE DISHES!" I **holler**ed to Mother and Daddy. "I'LL PUT OLLIE'S SWEATER ON HIS HEAD! 'CAUSE THAT WILL SAVE US TIME, I

THINK!"

I quick climbed into Ollie's **crib**.

Then I tried to pull that baby's sweater on him. Only his **giant** head didn't **fit** through the hole.

He waked up from his **nap**.

Then he started to cry very loud.

I heard loud feet running in the hall.

"JUNIE B. JONES! WHAT DO YOU THINK YOU ARE DOING?" yelled an angry voice.

It was Mother.

She runned in the room. And picked up baby Ollie.

She **pat**ted his giant head.

"That's quite a melon he has there," I said very quiet.

Baby Ollie kept on crying.

"Want me to get a **leash**?" I asked Mother. "Let's put him on a leash, okay? 'Cause he is all **jazz**ied **up**, I think. And so how will we even **control** him at the mall?"

Mother **roll**ed **her eyes** way back in her head.

"We're not *going* to the mall, Junie B.," she said. "We are not going anywhere."

I **stamp**ed my foot.

"Yes!" I said. "We *have* to! We *have* to go to the mall to get my princess dress! And my shoes with lightning. Or else that boy will not love me, I tell you!"

Mother closed her eyes. She did some deep breaths.

Her voice got softer.

"Okay. I want you to listen to me. And I want you to listen **careful**ly," she said. "You don't make friends by wearing new dresses or shoes with lightning. You make new friends by being fun to be with. And by being nice to people. And by caring about their feelings."

She **lift**ed me out of the crib.

"And *honesty* is important, too, Junie B.," she said. "You have to be *honest* with people. And that means that you can't **pretend** to be someone you're not."

She **smooth**ed my hair.

"You're *not* Lucille, Junie B. And you're not Grace, either. You're just *you*. You're just Junie B. Jones. And believe me, that's a big enough job for *anyone*."

I did a **sniffle**. Also I did a **snort** and a **swallow**.

"Yeah, only I *know* I am Junie B. Jones," I said. "I just want to be Junie B. Jones in a *princess* dress."

I put my head on her shoulder.

"Didn't you ever want a princess dress when you were a little girl?" I asked. "Huh, Mother? Didn't you?"

Mother didn't answer. She was **think**ing it **over** probably.

Just then, I looked over her **shoulder**.

I saw a new toy on baby Ollie's **shelf**.

"Hey! What's that, Mother? What's that on that shelf there? Is that a new teddy bear[2] I see?"

I runned and pulled that guy down.

"Look, Mother! Look what this bear is wearing! It is a ribbon made out of rich, red velvet! And that is *'zactly* the kind of cloth I've been looking for!"

I took the **bow** off the teddy. And I held it next to my hair.

"How do I look? Huh, Mother? Do I look like a beautiful princess? Do I look **gorgeous**? Huh? Do I?"

Just then, I felt happy and **sparkly** inside.

---

2 **teddy bear** 테디 베어. 장난감 곰 인형으로, 미국의 26대 대통령 테어 도어 루스벨트(Theodore Roosevelt)의 애칭을 따서 만들었다.

I quick kissed Mother and zoomed out of the room.

'Cause maybe there was more princess clothes right in my very own house!

6
Speechless

The next day, that Grace saw me on the bus.

Her mouth came **all the way** open.

I smiled very **gorgeous**.

"I know why you're looking at me like that, Grace," I said. "Mother said when people saw me, they would be speechless."

I **fluff**ed my hair.

"Speechless is when your mouth can't speech," I explained.

That Grace pointed at my neck.

"What is *that?* Is that a *dog* **collar** you're wearing?" she said.

I laughed and laughed at her.

"You **silly**head, Grace!" I said. "Don't you know anything? This is a **lovely** collar of **jewel**s! It is the kind of jewels that princesses wear! Only I didn't even know we had this gorgeous thing! I found it where Mother keeps the dog food. Only I don't actually know why it got put there."

I holded out my arms.

"And did you **notice** *these,* Grace? Did you notice my long white princess gloves? They are the kind of gloves that Cinderella[1] wears. And Cinderella is a real, actual princess. Plus also she does floors."

I pointed at my head.

"And what about this **golden crown** I am wearing? It is from a real actual Dairy Queen!² Plus, also I have red velvet **bow**s on my sneakers! And Mother even drew **lightning** on their sides. Just like yours!"

I **twirl**ed all around.

"Just wait till Handsome Warren **gets a load of** me now! Right, Grace? Now that guy will have to love me! 'Cause who wouldn't?"

Grace **slump**ed down in her seat.

---

1 **Cinderella** 신데렐라. 동화에 나오는 여주인공으로 계모와 계모의 딸들에게 구박을 받았는데 요정의 도움으로 궁중 무도회에 참석했다가 잃어버린 유리 구두 한 짝이 인연이 되어 왕자와 결혼한다.

2 **Dairy Queen** 데어리퀸. 미국의 대표적인 소프트아이스크림·패스트푸드 체인점이다. 컵에 담겨 거꾸로 뒤집어도 떨어지지 않는 아이스크림이 대표 메뉴이다.

She didn't talk the whole rest of the way to school.

And guess what else? When the bus got to school, she didn't even wait for me again.

She ran right straight to Handsome Warren without me.

I tried to **race** her. But my collar of jewels **scratch**ed my neck. Plus also my golden crown fell off my head.

Handsome Warren was sitting on the ground.

His face was hiding in his **knee**s.

I pushed my way in front of Lucille and that Grace.

Then I **tap**ped him on the head.

"Hello. How are you today? I am wearing princess clothes," I told him.

Handsome Warren didn't look up.

I tapped on his head again.

"Yeah, only I actually think you should get a load of me. 'Cause Grandma Miller says I am quite a **sight**," I said.

Lucille **roll**ed **her eyes**.

"It won't **do** you any **good** to talk to him, Junie B.," she said. "He's not talking to anyone."

"Not even to *me*," said that Grace.

I **squat**ted down next to that guy. And **stare**d real hard.

"How come you're not talking? Huh, Warren? Does the cat have your tongue?[3]"

---

3 **does the cat have your tongue?** 직역하면 '고양이가 혀를 물어갔나요?'라는 뜻으로, '왜 이렇게 말이 없나요?' 혹은 '왜 아무 말도 없나요?' 라고 물어볼 때 사용하는 숙어이다.

I waited very **patient**.

Then I **lean**ed closer to his ear.

"I SAID, DOES THE CAT HAVE YOUR TONGUE, WARREN?"

All of a sudden, Handsome Warren raised up his head.

"GO AWAY!" he shouted. "ALL OF YOU! GO AWAY AND LEAVE ME ALONE!"

I stayed squatted a real long time.

Then I stood up very quiet. And I looked at that Grace and Lucille.

"Good news," I said. "He talked."

After that, all of us kept on standing there and standing there.

'Cause we didn't actually know how to **handle** this situation, that's why.

Finally, Lucille did a **huffy** breath at him.

"You're not being nice, Warren. You used to be nice. But now you're not. And so I don't even want to be your friend today."

"Me, either," said that Grace. "I don't want to be your friend today, either!"

Then both of those guys held hands. And they **stomp**ed away from there very **furious**.

Handsome Warren raised up one **eyeball** to see if they were gone.

I quick **bend**ed down and looked into it.

"Hello. How are you today?" I said. "I am wearing princess clothes."

Handsome Warren did a **groan**.

Then he closed his eyeball. And he hided his face again.

7
Knock Knock

I sat down next to Handsome Warren.

"Guess what? I'm not even going to **bother** you," I said. "I'm just going to sit here. And mind my own **personal** beeswax. And **that's all.**"

I thought a little bit.

"Plus here's another good thing. You don't even have to look at my princess clothes if you don't want to. 'Cause clothes is not how I make friends," I said.

Handsome Warren didn't move.

I looked at his head.

"Guess what? There's something in your hair," I told him.

I looked harder at that thing.

"I think it's a **teeny** leaf. Or else maybe it's a piece of Kleenex,[1]" I said.

He still didn't move.

"Want me to **brush** it off for you?" I asked. "'Cause that would not be any trouble. And I would be happy to do it."

I waited very **patient** for him to answer.

Then I **tap**ped on him some more.

"Yeah, only I really think you should

---

1 **Kleenex** 크리넥스. 본래 휴지나 기저귀 등을 판매하는 미국의 생활용품 브랜드의 이름이지만, 화장지를 일컫는 일반적인 용어로 굳어졌다.

do something," I said. "'Cause what if somebody **blow**ed their nose on a teeny Kleenex? And then it flied in the wind. And got **stuck** in your hair. Did you ever think of that? Huh? 'Cause that would not be **pleasant**."

He didn't answer.

"Whoever wants me to get the Kleenex out of his hair, raise your hand," I said.

All of a sudden, Handsome Warren un**cover**ed his angry face.

"I thought you weren't going to talk!" he **holler**ed. "I thought you were going to mind your own personal beeswax!"

I smiled very cute.

"Yeah, only I *am* minding my own personal beeswax, Warren," I said. "I just needed to tell you about the teeny Kleenex. And so now I'm all done talking. **Period**. The end."

Handsome Warren **rolled his eyes** way up at the sky. He covered up with his arms again.

I waited some more.

"Okay, here's the problem," I said. "The teeny Kleenex is still there. And so how would you like me to **handle** this?"

Handsome Warren put his hands over his ears.

"Stop it!" he **yell**ed. "Stop talking to me! Why are you sitting here anyway? Why don't you just go with your stupid friends and leave me alone?"

"'Cause I am being nice, that's why," I

said. "Plus also I am understanding your feelings. **On account of** Mother said that is how I make friends."

Handsome Warren did a **grouchy** face.

"I'm *not* your friend," he said. "I don't have any friends at this school. All my friends were at my *other* school. But then my dad made me move here. And now nothing is the same. I hate this place! I hate it! I hate it!"

Then he quick hided his head in his **knee**s again. And he started to cry.

He tried to be quiet.

Only I still could hear him **sniffling** in there.

It made me feel sad inside.

I **pat**ted him very gentle.

"Sorry, Warren. Sorry you feel bad. Sorry. Sorry," I said real soft.

Just then a good idea **pop**ped in my head.

"Hey. *I* know. Maybe I can get you a Band-Aid.[2] Would you like that, Warren? 'Cause sometimes Band-Aids make things better . . .

"Or else here's another good idea. Maybe I could **tickle** you. 'Cause tickling makes you laugh, right? And so I would be glad to **give it a try**."

I **jiggle**d him.

"Want to try on my **golden crown**, Warren? Huh? Want to? 'Cause a golden

---

2 **Band-Aid** 반창고. 'Band-Aid'는 본래 미국 회사에서 사용하는 상표 명이었으나, 반창고를 일컫는 일반적인 용어로 굳어졌다.

crown makes you feel like a **million** bucks.[3]"

I took it off to give to him.

He didn't take it.

I put my golden crown on the ground.

Then I took off my princess **collar** and my Cinderella gloves. And I put them on the ground, too.

After that, I sat very **still**. And I listened to Warren being sad.

Finally I did a **sigh**. And I tried my very last idea.

"Knock knock," I said.

Handsome Warren didn't answer.

"Knock knock," I said a little bit louder.

---

3 **buck** 미국이나 호주, 뉴질랜드의 달러를 이르는 비격식적인 표현.

Then I kept on saying knock knock, until that guy got sick of it.

"OH, ALL RIGHT! WHO'S THERE?" he **grouch**ed.

"Hatch,[4]" I said.

"Hatch who?" said Handsome Warren.

"HA HA! MADE YOU **SNEEZE**! GET IT, WARREN? GET IT? YOU SAID *HATCHOO!* DO YOU GET IT?

"Knock knock," I said again.

Handsome Warren **peek**ed one eye at me.

"Who's there?" he said.

"Ash,[4]" I said.

---

4 **hatch, ash** 여기에서는 본래의 뜻이 아니라, 재채기와 비슷한 소리를 내도록 하는 언어유희로 쓰였다. 이 책에 나오는 'kook'은 'cuckoo'로, 'icy'는 'I see'로, 그리고 'Irish'는 'I wish'로 연결되는 언어유희이다.

"Ash who?" said Handsome Warren.

"HA! I DID IT AGAIN, WARREN! I MADE YOU SNEEZE AGAIN! YOU SAID *ASHOO!* AND SO THAT WAS ANOTHER GOOD ONE, RIGHT?"

Handsome Warren raised up his head. His face didn't look as mad.

"Knock knock," I said.

"Who's there?" said Handsome Warren.

"Kook."

"Kook who?" he said.

I made a **fist** at that guy.

"Hey! Who are you calling cuckoo, mister?" I said.

Just then, Handsome Warren did a teeny smile.

He waited for a second. Then he smiled

some more.

"Knock knock," he said.

"Who's there?"

"Icy," said Handsome Warren.

"Icy who?"

"Icy London, Icy France, Icy Lucille's **underpants**," he said.

I **clap**ped and clapped.

"Me too, Warren! I saw those things, too! 'Cause that crazy kook is always **twirl**ing around in those **bouncy** dresses, that's why!"

All of a sudden, my whole face **light**ed up.

"Knock knock!"

"Who's there?" said Handsome Warren.

"Irish."

"Irish who?"

"IRISH I WAS AN OSCAR MAYER WIENER!^{5}" I sang real loud.

Then me and Handsome Warren started laughing real hard! And we holded our **sides**! And we **roll**ed all around on the ground!

"YOU ARE A NUTBALL!" said Handsome Warren.

"YOU ARE A NUTBALL, TOO!" I said back.

"WE ARE *BOTH* NUTBALLS!" he said.

And so after that, me and Nutball Warren rolled and laughed and rolled and

---

5 **Oscar Mayer Wiener song** 햄이나 소시지 등을 판매하는 미국의 육가공품 회사 Oscar Mayer가 핫도그를 만들 때 사용하는 프랑크푸르트 소시지(wiener)를 홍보하기 위해 만든 광고 노래. 여기에서 'I wish I were an Oscar Mayer Wiener'라는 말은 노래 가사의 일부이다.

laughed. All around the grass. Till the bell
rang!

'Cause that's what nutballs do, of
course!

Plus also me and him were **brand-new**

friends, I think!

And that is called *happily ever after!*

junie b. jones®

주니 B. 존스는
잘생긴 위런을 좋아해

junie b. jones®

주니 B. 존스는
잘생긴 위런을 좋아해

by **BARBARA PARK**

illustrated by
Denise Brunkus

CONTENTS

세상에서 가장 엉뚱하고 재미있는 아이, 주니 B. 존스의 좌충우돌 성장기!

『주니 B. 존스(Junie B. Jones)』시리즈는 호기심 많은 개구쟁이 소녀 주니 B.가 일상에서 마주하는 다양한 상황을 재치 있게 담고 있습니다. 주니 B.는 언제나 자신의 감정을 솔직하게 표현하며, 재미있는 생각이 떠오르면 주저없이 실행에 옮기는 적극적인 여섯 살 소녀입니다. 이렇게 유쾌하고 재기 발랄한 주니 B. 존스의 성장기는 지금까지 전 세계적으로 6천 5백만 부 이상 판매되며 수많은 독자들에게 사랑받았고, 연극과 뮤지컬로 제작되기도 했습니다.

저자 바바라 파크(Barbara Park)는 첫 등교, 친구 관계, 동생에 대한 고민 등과 같이 일상 속 다양한 상황에서 아이들이 느끼는 감정을 그들의 시선으로 탁월하게 묘사했습니다. 특히 아이들이 영어로 말할 때 저지르기 쉬운 실수도 자연스럽게 녹여 내어, 이야기에 더욱 공감하게 합니다.

이러한 이유로『주니 B. 존스』시리즈는 '엄마표 영어'를 진행하는 부모님과 초보 영어 학습자에게 반드시 읽어야 할 영어원서로 자리 잡았습니다. 친근한 어휘와 쉬운 문장으로 쓰여 있어 더욱 몰입하여 읽을 수 있는『주니 B. 존스』시리즈는 영어원서가 친숙하지 않은 학습자들에게도 즐거운 원서 읽기 경험을 선사할 것입니다.

퀴즈와 단어장, 그리고 번역까지 담긴 알찬 구성의 워크북!

이 책은 영어원서『주니 B. 존스』시리즈에, 탁월한 학습 효과를 거둘 수 있도록 다양한 콘텐츠를 덧붙인 책입니다.

- 영어원서: 본문에 나온 어려운 어휘에 볼드 처리가 되어 있어 단어를 더욱 분명히 인지하며 자연스럽게 암기하게 됩니다.
- 단어장: 원서에 나온 어려운 어휘가 '한영'은 물론 '영영' 의미까지 완벽하게 정리되어 있으며, 반복되는 단어까지 표시하여 자연스럽게 복습이 되도록 구성했습니다.
- 번역: 영어와 비교할 수 있도록 직역에 가까운 번역을 담았습니다. 원서 읽기에 익숙하지 않은 초보 학습자도 어려움 없이 내용을 파악할 수 있습니다.
- 퀴즈: 챕터별로 내용을 확인하는 이해력 점검 퀴즈가 들어 있습니다.

『주니 B. 존스』, 이렇게 읽어 보세요!

● **단어 암기는 이렇게!** 처음 리딩을 시작하기 전, 해당 챕터에 나오는 단어를 눈으로 쭉 훑어봅니다. 모르는 단어는 좀 더 주의 깊게 보되, 손으로 쓰면서 완벽하게 암기할 필요는 없습니다. 본문을 읽으면서 이 단어를 다시 만나게 되는데, 그 과정에서 단어의 쓰임새와 어감을 자연스럽게 익히게 됩니다. 이렇게 책을 읽은 후에, 단어를 다시 한번 복습하세요. 복습할 때는 중요하다고 생각하는 단어들을 손으로 쓰면서 꼼꼼하게 외우는 것도 좋습니다. 이런 방식으로 책을 읽다 보면, 많은 단어를 빠르고 부담 없이 익히게 됩니다.

● **리딩할 때는 리딩에만 집중하자!** 원서를 읽는 중간중간 모르는 단어가 나온다고 워크북을 들춰 보거나, 곧바로 번역을 찾아보는 것은 매우 좋지 않은 습관입니다. 모르는 단어나 이해가 가지 않는 문장이 나온다고 해도 펜으로 가볍게 표시만 해 두고, 전체적인 맥락을 잡아 가며 빠르게 읽어 나가세요. 리딩을 할 때는 속도에 대한 긴장감을 잃지 않으면서 리딩에만 집중하는 것이 좋습니다. 모르는 단어와 문장은, 리딩이 끝난 후에 한꺼번에 정리하는 '리뷰' 시간을 통해 점검합니다. 리뷰를 할 때는 번역은 물론 단어장과 사전도 꼼꼼하게 확인하면서 왜 이해가 되지 않았는지 확인해 봅니다.

● **번역 활용은 이렇게!** 이해가 가지 않는 문장은 번역을 통해서 그 의미를 파악할 수 있습니다. 하지만 한국어와 영어는 정확히 1:1 대응이 되지 않기 때문에 번역을 활용하는 데에도 지혜가 필요합니다. 의역이 된 부분까지 억지로 의미를 대응해서 암기하려고 하기보다, 어떻게 그런 의미가 만들어진 것인지 추측하면서 번역은 참고 자료로 활용하는 것이 좋습니다.

● **2~3번 반복해서 읽자!** 영어 초보자라면 2~3회 반복해서 읽을 것을 추천합니다. 초보자일수록 처음 읽을 때는 생소한 단어와 스토리 때문에 내용 파악에 급급할 수밖에 없습니다. 하지만 일단 내용을 파악한 후에 다시 읽으면 어휘와 문장 구조 등 다른 부분까지 관찰하면서 조금 더 깊이 있게 읽을 수 있고, 그 과정에서 리딩 속도도 빨라지고 리딩 실력을 더 확고하게 다지게 됩니다.

- **'시리즈'로 꾸준히 읽자!** 한 작가의 책을 시리즈로 읽는 것 또한 영어 실력 향상에 큰 도움이 됩니다. 같은 등장인물이 다시 나오기 때문에 내용 파악이 더 수월할 뿐 아니라, 작가가 사용하는 어휘와 표현들도 자연스럽게 반복되기 때문에 탁월한 복습 효과까지 얻을 수 있습니다. 『주니 B. 존스』시리즈는 현재 8권, 총 52,646단어 분량이 출간되어 있습니다. 시리즈를 꾸준히 읽다 보면 영어 실력도 자연스럽게 향상될 것입니다.

영어원서 본문 구성

내용이 담긴 본문입니다.

원어민이 읽는 일반 원서와 같은 텍스트지만, 암기해야 할 중요 어휘는 볼드체로 표시되어 있습니다. 이 어휘들은 지금 들고 계신 워크북에 챕터별로 정리되어 있습니다.

학습 심리학 연구 결과에 따르면, 한 단어씩 따로 외우는 단어 암기는 거의 효과가 없다고 합니다. 대신 단어를 제대로 외우기 위해서는 문맥(Context) 속에서 단어를 암기해야 하며, 한 단어 당 문맥 속에서 15번 이상 마주칠 때 완벽하게 암기할 수 있다고 합니다.

이 책의 본문은 중요 어휘를 볼드로 강조하여, 문맥 속의 단어들을 더 확실히 인지(Word Cognition in Context)하도록 돕고 있습니다. 또한 대부분의 중요한 단어는 다른 챕터에서도 반복해서 등장하기 때문에 이 책을 읽는 것만으로도 자연스럽게 어휘력을 향상시킬 수 있습니다.

또한 본문에는 내용 이해를 돕기 위해 '각주'가 첨가되어 있습니다. 각주는 굳이 암기할 필요는 없지만, 알아 두면 내용을 더 깊이 있게 이해할 수 있어 원서를 읽는 재미가 배가됩니다.

JUNIE B. JONES

워크북(Workbook)의 구성

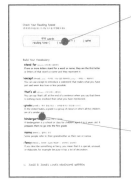

Check Your Reading Speed
해당 챕터의 단어 수가 기록되어 있어, 리딩 속도를 측정할 수 있습니다. 특히 리딩 속도를 중시하는 독자는 유용하게 사용할 수 있습니다.

Build Your Vocabulary
본문에 볼드 표시되어 있는 단어가 정리되어 있습니다. 리딩 전, 후에 반복해서 보면 원서를 더욱 쉽게 읽을 수 있고, 어휘력도 빠르게 향상됩니다.

단어는 〈빈도 ─ 스펠링 ─ 발음기호 ─ 품사 ─ 한국어 뜻 ─ 영어 뜻〉 순서로 표기되어 있으며 빈도 표시(★)가 많을수록 필수 어휘입니다. 반복해서 등장하는 단어는 빈도 대신 '복습'으로 표기되어 있습니다. 품사는 아래와 같이 표기했습니다.

n. 명사 l a. 형용사 l ad. 부사 l v. 동사
conj. 접속사 l prep. 전치사 l int. 감탄사 l idiom 숙어 및 관용구

Comprehension Quiz
간단한 퀴즈를 통해 읽은 내용에 대한 이해력을 점검해 볼 수 있습니다.

번역
영문과 비교할 수 있도록 최대한 직역에 가까운 번역을 담았습니다.

이 책의 수준과 타깃 독자

- **미국 원어민 기준**: 유치원 ~ 초등학교 저학년
- **한국 학습자 기준**: 초등학교 저학년 ~ 중학생
- **영어원서 완독 경험이 없는 초보 영어 학습자** (토익 기준 450~750 점대)
- **비슷한 수준의 다른 챕터북**: Arthur Chapter Book, Flat Stanley, The Zack Files, Magic Tree House, Marvin Redpost
- **도서 분량**: 약 6,000단어

아이도 어른도 재미있게 읽는 영어원서를
〈롱테일 에디션〉으로 만나 보세요!

아서 챕터북 시리즈

플랫 스탠리 시리즈

Chapter
1

1. Why did Junie B. and Grace look for Lucille?

  A. They wanted to see her new bow.

  B. They wanted to ask about her parrot.

  C. They wanted to chase her.

  D. They wanted to play with her.

2. Why did Junie B. and Grace shoo the boy away?

  A. They thought that he was running too fast.

  B. They thought that he was bothering Lucille.

  C. They thought that he was breaking the rules.

  D. They thought that he liked Lucille.

3. **Why was Lucille angry that Junie B. and Grace shooed the boy away?**

   A. She was close friends with him.

   B. She was trying to talk to him.

   C. She liked the attention from him.

   D. She was planning to watch TV with him.

4. **How did Junie B. start to feel about Warren?**

   A. She thought that he looked smart.

   B. She thought that he looked familiar.

   C. She was not impressed by him.

   D. She was interested in him.

5. **Why didn't Lucille think that her friends should have a chance with Warren?**

   A. They would steal him from her.

   B. Junie B. stole her last boyfriend.

   C. Grace was not as beautiful as she was.

   D. They had never seen Warren's commercial.

$$\frac{977 \text{ words}}{\text{reading time ( ) sec}} \times 60 = (\qquad) \text{ wPM}$$

Build Your Vocabulary

stand for idiom 나타내다; 옹호하다
If one or more letters stand for a word or name, they are the first letter or letters of that word or name and they represent it.

except [iksépt] conj. ~이지만; ~라는 점만 제외하면; prep. ~ 외에는; v. 제외하다
You can use except to introduce a statement that makes what you have just said seem less true or less possible.

that's all idiom 그게 다이다, 그뿐이다
You can say 'that's all' at the end of a sentence when you say that there is nothing more involved than what you have mentioned.

grade [greid] n. 학년; 품질; 등급; v. 성적을 매기다; (등급을) 나누다
In the United States, a grade is a group of classes in which all the children are of a similar age.

kindergarten [kíndərgàːrtn] n. 유치원
A kindergarten is a school or class for children aged 4 to 6 years old. It prepares them to go into the first grade.

nanna [nǽnə] n. 할머니; 유모
Some people refer to their grandmother as their nan or nanna.

fancy [fǽnsi] a. 화려한; 고급의; 복잡한; v. 생각하다, 상상하다
If you describe something as fancy, you mean that it is special, unusual, or elaborate, for example because it has a lot of decoration.

lacy [léisi] a. 레이스의, 레이스 같은
Lacy things are made from lace or have pieces of lace attached to them.

‡ride [raid] v. (말·차량 등을) 타다; n. (말·차량 등을) 타고 달리기
When you ride a vehicle such as a car, you travel in it, especially as a passenger.

∗automatic [ɔ̀:təmǽtik] a. 자동의; 무의식적인 (automatically ad. 자동적으로)
If something happens automatically, it happens as part of the normal process or system.

∗curly [kə́:rli] a. 곱슬곱슬한
Curly hair is full of curving shapes, like part of a circle.

race [reis] n. 경주; 인종, 종족; v. 경주하다; 쏜살같이 가다; (머리·심장 등이) 바쁘게 돌아가다
A race is a competition to see who is the fastest, for example in running, swimming, or driving.

‡sport [spɔːrt] n. 너그러운 사람, 쾌활한 사람; 스포츠, 운동; v. 자랑스럽게 보이다
If you say that someone is a sport or a good sport, you mean that they cope with a difficult situation or teasing in a cheerful way.

‡cheat [tʃiːt] v. 속이다, 사기 치다; 부정행위를 하다; n. 사기꾼; 속임수 (cheater n. 사기꾼)
A cheater is someone who behaves in a dishonest way.

∗gallop [gǽləp] v. 전속력으로 달리다, 질주하다; n. 전속력으로 말을 몰기; 질주
When a horse gallops, it runs very fast so that all four legs are off the ground at the same time.

∗trot [trat] v. 빨리 걷다; 종종걸음을 걷다; n. 속보, 빠른 걸음
When an animal such as a horse trots, it moves fairly fast, taking quick small steps.

∗snort [snɔːrt] v. (말이) 코를 힝힝거리다; 코웃음을 치다, 콧방귀를 뀌다;
n. (말이) 코를 힝힝거리는 소리; 코웃음, 콧방귀
When people or animals snort, they breathe air noisily out through their noses.

★ **tap** [tæp] v. (가볍게) 톡톡 두드리다; n. (가볍게) 두드리기

If you tap something, you hit it with a quick light blow or a series of quick light blows.

‡ **chin** [ʧin] n. 턱

Your chin is the part of your face that is below your mouth and above your neck.

★ **parrot** [pǽrət] n. [동물] 앵무새

A parrot is a tropical bird with a curved beak and brightly-colored or grey feathers. Some parrots are able to copy what people say.

★ **tangle** [tæŋgl] v. 얽히다, 헝클어지다; n. (실·머리카락 등이) 엉킨 것; (혼란스럽게) 꼬인 상태

If something is tangled or tangles, it becomes twisted together in a messy way.

real live [ríːəl làiv] a. 실물의, 진짜의

You use real live to say that someone or something is present or exists, when you want to indicate that you think this is exciting and unusual or unexpected.

teeny [tíːni] a. 아주 작은

If you describe something as teeny, you are emphasizing that it is very small.

★ **bald** [bɔːld] a. 머리가 벗겨진, 대머리의

Someone who is bald or baldy has little or no hair on the top of their head.

‡ **spot** [spat] n. (특정한) 곳; (작은) 점; v. 발견하다, 찾다, 알아채다

You can refer to a particular place as a spot.

★ **bow** [bou] ① n. 나비매듭 리본; 활 ② n. (고개 숙여 하는) 인사; 절; v. (허리를 굽혀) 절하다

A bow is a knot with two loops and two loose ends that is used in tying shoelaces and ribbons.

‡ **curious** [kjúəriəs] a. 궁금한, 호기심이 많은; 별난, 특이한, 기이한

If you are curious about something, you are interested in it and want to know more about it.

gulp [gʌlp] n. 꿀꺽 삼키기; v. 꿀꺽꿀꺽 삼키다; (숨을) 깊이 들이마시다
A gulp means an act of breathing in or of swallowing something.

pretend [priténd] v. ~인 척하다, ~인 것처럼 굴다; ~라고 가장하다
If you pretend that something is the case, you act in a way that is intended to make people believe that it is the case, although in fact it is not.

water fountain [wɔ́:tər fàuntən] n. (분수식) 식수대
A water fountain is a machine in a park or other public place that provides drinking water when you push a button.

chase [ʧeis] v. 뒤쫓다, 추적하다; 추구하다; n. 추적, 추격; 추구함
If you chase someone, or chase after them, you run after them or follow them quickly in order to catch or reach them.

yell [jel] v. 고함치다, 소리 지르다; n. 고함, 외침
If you yell, you shout loudly, usually because you are excited, angry, or in pain.

squint [skwint] v. 눈을 가늘게 뜨고 보다; 곁눈질로 보다; n. 잠깐 봄; 사시
If you squint at something, you look at it with your eyes partly closed.

evil [í:vəl] a. 사악한, 악랄한; 유해한; 악마의; n. 악
If you describe someone as evil, you mean that they are very wicked by nature and take pleasure in doing things that harm other people.

wave [weiv] v. (손·팔을) 흔들다; 손짓하다; 흔들리다; n. (손·팔·몸을) 흔들기; 파도, 물결
If you wave or wave your hand, you move your hand from side to side in the air, usually in order to say hello or goodbye to someone.

spring [spriŋ] v. (sprang/sprung-sprung) 휙 움직이다; 튀다; n. 생기, 활기; 봄
(spring into action idiom 즉각 행동을 개시하다)
If you spring into action, you suddenly start working or doing something.

catch up idiom 따라잡다, 따라가다
If you catch up with someone, you go faster so that you reach them in front of you.

speedy [spíːdi] a. 빠른, 신속한
A speedy process, event, or action happens or is done very quickly.

shoo [ʃuː] v. 쉬이 하고 쫓아내다; 쉬이 하다; int. 쉬, 쉬이 (새 등을 쫓는 소리)
If you shoo an animal or a person away, you make them go away by waving your hands or arms at them.

tell on idiom ~를 고자질하다
If you tell on someone, you give information about them to a person in authority, especially if they have done something wrong.

principal [prínsəpəl] n. 교장; a. 주요한, 주된
The principal of a school or college is the person in charge of the school or college.

personal [pə́rsənl] a. 개인적인, 개인의
A personal relationship is one that is not connected with your job or public life.

pound [paund] v. (여러 차례) 두드리다; (가슴이) 쿵쿵 뛰다; 쿵쾅거리며 걷다
If you pound something or pound on it, you hit it with great force, usually loudly and repeatedly.

high five [hài fáiv] n. 하이 파이브
If you give someone a high five, you put your hand up and hit their open hand with yours, especially after a victory or as a greeting.

hurray [həréi] int. 만세
People sometimes shout 'Hurray!' when they are very happy and excited about something.

all of a sudden idiom 갑자기
If something happens all of a sudden, it happens quickly and unexpectedly.

stomp [stamp] v. 쿵쿵거리며 걷다; 발을 구르며 춤추다
If you stomp somewhere, you walk there with very heavy steps, often because you are angry.

holler [hálər] v. 소리 지르다, 고함치다; n. 고함, 외침
If you holler, you shout loudly.

‡ **ruin** [rúːin] v. 엉망으로 만들다; 폐허로 만들다; n. 붕괴, 몰락; 파멸
To ruin something means to severely harm, damage, or spoil it.

‡‡ **proud** [praud] a. 자랑스러워하는, 자랑스러운; 오만한, 거만한
If you feel proud, you feel pleased about something good that you possess or have done, or about something good that a person close to you has done.

‡ **commercial** [kəmə́ːrʃəl] n. (텔레비전·라디오의) 광고; a. 상업의; 상업적인
A commercial is an advertisement that is broadcast on television or radio.

★ **eyebrow** [áibràu] n. 눈썹
Your eyebrows are the lines of hair which grow above your eyes.

tiptoe [típtòu] n. (= tippy-toe) 발끝, 까치발; v. 발끝으로 (살금살금) 걷다
If you do something on tiptoe or on tiptoes, you do it standing or walking on the front part of your foot, without putting your heels on the ground.

‡ **practical** [præktikəl] a. 거의 완전한, 사실상의; 현실적인 (practically ad. 거의, 사실상)
Practically means almost, but not completely or exactly.

★ **pop** [pap] v. 눈이 휘둥그레지다; 불쑥 나타나다; 펑 하는 소리가 나다; n. 펑 (하는 소리)
If your eyes pop or pop out, they suddenly open fully because you are surprised or excited.

★ **chunk** [ʧʌŋk] n. 체격이 큰 사람; 상당히 많은 양; 덩어리; v. 덩어리로 나누다
If you describe someone as a chunk, you mean that they are thick-set and strong.

think over idiom ~을 심사숙고하다
If you think something over, you consider it carefully, especially before making a decision.

‡ **careful** [kéərfəl] a. 신중한, 조심하는, 주의 깊은; 세심한
If you are careful, you give serious attention to what you are doing, in order to avoid harm, damage, or mistakes.

✲ crack [kræk] n. 도전(의 기회); (갈라져 생긴) 금; (좁은) 틈; v. 갈라지게 하다; 깨뜨리다
If you have or take a crack at something, you make an attempt to do or achieve something.

✲ definite [défənit] a. 확실한, 확고한; 분명한, 뚜렷한 (definitely ad. 확실히, 분명히)
You use definitely to emphasize that something is the case, or to emphasize the strength of your intention or opinion.

✲ stamp [stæmp] v. (발을) 구르다; 쾅쾅거리며 걷다; (도장 등을) 찍다; n. (발을) 쿵쾅거리기; 도장
If you stamp or stamp your foot, you lift your foot and put it down very hard on the ground, for example because you are angry.

✲ steal [sti:l] v. 훔치다, 도둑질하다; 살며시 움직이다
If you steal something from someone, you take it away from them without their permission and without intending to return it.

✲ fair [fɛər] a. 공정한; 타당한; 아름다운; ad. 공정하게, 타당하게; n. 축제; 박람회
Something or someone that is fair is reasonable, right, and just.

peek [pi:k] n. 엿보기; v. (재빨리) 훔쳐보다; 살짝 보이다
If you take a peek at someone or something, you have a quick look at them, often secretly.

move on idiom (새로운 일·주제로) 옮기다, 넘어가다
If you move on, you finish or stop one activity and start doing something different.

boiling mad idiom 몹시 화가 난, 미친 듯이 흥분한
Someone who is boiling mad is extremely angry.

Chapter
2

1. **Why did Junie B. show her socks to Lucille?**

   A. To show that her feet were fancy

   B. To make Lucille feel sorry for her

   C. To prove that she could not steal Warren

   D. To explain how bad her dog was

2. **What did Junie B. yell to Grace in class?**

   A. Lucille would consider introducing them to Warren.

   B. Lucille would mention their names to Warren.

   C. Lucille would be best friends with them again.

   D. Lucille would forgive them for making her mad.

3. What did Mrs. tell Junie B.?

A. She was being too loud.

B. She still had a lot of work to finish.

C. Making a fist at other kids was mean.

D. Standing up on her chair was dangerous.

4. What did Junie B. think about herself and Grace?

A. They were just like pigs.

B. They were not really like pigs.

C. They were better than Lucille.

D. They were not as good as Lucille.

5. How did Warren react when he met Junie B.?

A. He called her weird.

B. He laughed at her joke.

C. He said that she was fun.

D. He would not even look at her.

1분에 몇 단어를 읽는지 리딩 속도를 측정해 보세요.

$$\frac{864 \text{ words}}{\text{reading time ( ) sec}} \times 60 = (\quad) \text{ wPM}$$

Build Your Vocabulary

^{복습} **steal** [stiːl] v. 훔치다, 도둑질하다; 살며시 움직이다
If you steal something from someone, you take it away from them without their permission and without intending to return it.

fluff [flʌf] v. 부풀리다; n. (동물이나 새의) 솜털; 보풀
If you fluff something, you shake or brush it so that it looks larger and softer.

^{복습} **lacy** [léisi] a. 레이스의, 레이스 같은
Lacy things are made from lace or have pieces of lace attached to them.

✱ **include** [inklúːd] v. 포함하다; ~을 (~에) 포함시키다
If one thing includes another thing, it has the other thing as one of its parts.

✱ **tax** [tæks] n. 세금; v. 세금을 부과하다, 과세하다
Tax is an amount of money that you have to pay to the government so that it can pay for public services.

bug out idiom 눈이 휘둥그레지다
If someone's eyes bug out, they open very wide, for example because the person is shocked by something.

^{복습} **fancy** [fǽnsi] a. 화려한; 고급의; 복잡한; v. 생각하다, 상상하다
If you describe something as fancy, you mean that it is special, unusual, or elaborate, for example because it has a lot of decoration.

sag [sæg] v. 축 처지다, 축 늘어지다; 약화되다, 줄어들다; n. 늘어짐, 처짐
When something sags, it hangs down loosely or sinks downward in the middle.

droopy [drúːpi] a. 축 늘어진; 지친, 의기소침한
If you describe something as droopy, you mean that it hangs or leans downward with no strength or firmness.

⋆ **tug** [tʌg] n. (갑자기 세게) 잡아당김; v. (세게) 잡아당기다
You can refer to a short strong pull as a tug.

drooly [drúːli] a. 침을 흘리는
If you describe a person or animal as drooly, saliva drops slowly from their mouth.

make a face idiom 얼굴을 찌푸리다, 침울한 표정을 짓다
If you make a face, you show a feeling such as dislike or disgust by putting an exaggerated expression on your face.

scoot [skuːt] v. 휙 움직이다; 서둘러 가다
If you scoot someone or something, you make them move a short distance by pulling or pushing.

⋆ **clap** [klæp] v. 박수를 치다; (갑자기·재빨리) 놓다; n. 박수; 쿵 하는 소리
When you clap, you hit your hands together to show appreciation or attract attention.

⋆ **thrill** [θril] v. 열광시키다, 정말 신나게 하다; n. 흥분, 설렘; 전율 (**thrilled** a. 아주 신이 난)
If someone is thrilled, they are extremely pleased about something.

복습 **holler** [hálər] v. 소리 지르다, 고함치다; n. 고함, 외침
If you holler, you shout loudly.

복습 **that's all** idiom 그게 다이다, 그뿐이다
You can say 'that's all' at the end of a sentence when you say that there is nothing more involved than what you have mentioned.

meanie [míːni] n. 심술쟁이, 쩨쩨한 사람
A meanie is used especially by children to describe someone who is unkind, unpleasant, or not generous.

* **fist** [fist] n. 주먹
Your hand is referred to as your fist when you have bent your fingers in toward the palm in order to hit someone, to make an angry gesture, or to hold something.

* **entire** [intáiər] a. 전체의, 완전한, 온전한
You use entire when you want to emphasize that you are referring to the whole of something, for example, the whole of a place, time, or population.

plop [plap] v. 털썩 주저앉다; 떨어뜨리다; 퐁당 하고 떨어지다; n. 퐁당 (하는 소리)
If someone plops or you plop them, they sit down or land heavily or without taking care.

grouch [grautʃ] v. 불평하다; 토라지다; n. 불평; 불평꾼
To grouch means to complain a lot, often without good reason.

‡ **mean** [miːn] v. ~할 작정으로 말하다; 의미하다; a. 못된, 심술궂은
If you say that you mean what you are saying, you are telling someone that you are serious about it and are not joking, exaggerating, or just being polite.

‡ **spell** [spel] v. (어떤 단어의) 철자를 쓰다; 철자를 맞게 쓰다; n. 주문; 마법
(spelling n. 철자 쓰기; 철자)
Spelling is an attempt to write or speak each letter in a word in the correct order.

* **arithmetic** [əríθmətik] n. 산수, 연산; 산술, 계산
Arithmetic is the part of mathematics that is concerned with the addition, subtraction, multiplication, and division of numbers.

‡ **print** [print] v. (글자를) 인쇄체로 쓰다; 인쇄하다; n. (인쇄된) 활자
If you print words, you write in letters that are not joined together and that look like the letters in a book or newspaper.

✳ assignment [əsáinmənt] n. 과제, 임무
An assignment is a task or piece of work that you are given to do, especially as part of your job or studies.

✳ recess [risés] n. (학교의) 쉬는 시간; (의회·위원회 등의) 휴회 기간
A recess is a short period of time during the school day when children can play.

✳ trample [trǽmpl] v. 짓밟다, 밟아 뭉개다; (남의 감정·권리를) 짓밟다
If someone tramples something or tramples on it, they step heavily and carelessly on it and damage it.

✳ neighbor [néibər] n. 옆자리 사람; 이웃 (사람); v. 이웃하다, 인접하다
You can refer to the person who is standing or sitting next to you as your neighbor.

✳ upset [ʌpsét] a. 속상한, 마음이 상한; v. 속상하게 하다
If you are upset, you are unhappy or disappointed because something unpleasant has happened to you.

✳ whisper [hwíspər] v. 속삭이다, 소곤거리다; n. 속삭임, 소곤거리는 소리
When you whisper, you say something very quietly, using your breath rather than your throat, so that only one person can hear you.

✳ giant [dʒáiənt] a. 거대한, 엄청나게 큰; 비범한; n. 거인
Something that is described as giant is extremely large, strong, powerful, or important.

stink [stiŋk] n. 악취; v. (고약한) 냄새가 나다, 악취가 풍기다; 수상쩍다
Stink means a strong unpleasant smell.

✳ hog [hɔːg] n. [동물] 돼지; v. 독차지하다
A hog is a pig.

✳ skip [skip] v. 깡충깡충 뛰다; (일을) 거르다; 생략하다; n. 깡충깡충 뛰기
If you skip along, you move almost as if you are dancing, with a series of little jumps from one foot to the other.

⚝ **swing** [swiŋ] n. 그네; 흔들기; v. (전후·좌우로) 흔들다, 흔들리다; 획 움직이다; 휘두르다
(swing set n. 그네와 미끄럼틀 세트)
A swing set is a frame for children to play on including one or more swings and often a slide.

⚝ **all of a sudden** idiom 갑자기
If something happens all of a sudden, it happens quickly and unexpectedly.

⭐ **grab** [græb] v. (와락·단단히) 붙잡다; 급히 ~하다; n. 와락 잡아채려고 함
If you grab someone or something, you take or hold them with your hand suddenly, firmly, or roughly.

⚝ **wave** [weiv] v. (손·팔을) 흔들다; 손짓하다; 흔들리다; n. (팔·손·몸을) 흔들기; 파도, 물결
If you wave or wave your hand, you move your hand from side to side in the air, usually in order to say hello or goodbye to someone.

⚝ **friendly** [fréndli] a. (행동이) 친절한; 우호적인; 사용하기 편한
If someone is friendly, they behave in a pleasant, kind way, and like to be with other people.

⭐ **shy** [ʃai] a. 수줍음을 많이 타는, 수줍어하는
A shy person is nervous and uncomfortable in the company of other people.

⚝ **peek** [piːk] v. (재빨리) 훔쳐보다; 살짝 보이다; n. 엿보기
If you peek at someone or something, you have a quick look at them, often secretly.

⚝ **joke** [dʒouk] n. 농담; 웃음거리; v. 농담하다; 농담 삼아 말하다
A joke is something that is said or done to make you laugh, such as a funny story.

⚝ **control** [kəntróul] n. 통제, 제어; 지배; v. 통제하다; 지배하다; 조정하다
(out of control idiom 통제 불능의)
If someone or something is out of control, they are or become impossible to manage or to control.

⁑side [said] n. (사람 몸통의) 옆구리; 옆; (한) 쪽
Your sides are the parts of your body between your front and your back, from under your arms to your hips.

⁑roll [roul] v. 구르다, 굴러가다; 굴리다; n. (둥글게 말아 놓은) 통, 두루마리
If you are lying down and you roll over, you turn your body so that a different part of you is facing upward.

Chapter
3

1. What did Grace say to Lucille?

A. She loved Warren more than anyone else did.

B. She could not stop Warren from loving her.

C. She could steal any boy that she wanted.

D. She never meant to fall in love with Warren.

2. What did Lucille want Junie B. to do?

A. Tell Warren that he should choose one girl

B. Tell Warren that he made Junie B. feel bad

C. Tell Grace that friendship was more important than boys

D. Tell Grace that she could not take Warren away

3. Why didn't Junie B. talk for the rest of the school day?

A. She kept thinking about what Warren said.

B. She did not want to talk about Warren anymore.

C. She was tired from laughing so much at recess.

D. She had nothing special to say to her friends.

4. What did Junie B. say on the bus?

A. She did not know what a nutball was.

B. She did not think that Warren liked nutballs.

C. She did not understand how she was a nutball.

D. She did not care about being a nutball.

5. What was true about Grace's brother?

A. He was no longer a nutball.

B. He ate cereal every day.

C. He could be hard to control.

D. He loved going to the mall.

Check Your Reading Speed

1분에 몇 단어를 읽는지 리딩 속도를 측정해 보세요.

$$\frac{787 \text{ words}}{\text{reading time ( ) sec}} \times 60 = (\qquad) \text{ wPM}$$

Build Your Vocabulary

✻ **blow** [blou] v. (blew-blown) (입으로) 불다; (바람·입김에) 날리다; 폭파하다; n. 강타
If you blow, you send out a stream of air from your mouth.

✻ **whistle** [hwisl] n. 호루라기 (소리); 쌕쌕 소리; v. 휘파람을 불다; 쌕쌕 소리를 내다
A whistle is a small metal tube that you blow in order to produce a loud sound and attract someone's attention.

recess [risés] n. (학교의) 쉬는 시간; (의회·위원회 등의) 휴회 기간
A recess is a short period of time during the school day when children can play.

sparkly [spá:rkli] a. 활기 있는, 생기에 찬; 반짝반짝 빛나는
If you describe someone as sparkly, you mean that they are lively and witty.

twirl [twə:rl] v. 빙글빙글 돌다, 빙글빙글 돌리다; 빙빙 돌리다; n. 회전
If you twirl, you turn around and around quickly, for example when you are dancing.

squeal [skwi:l] v. 꽥 하는 소리를 내다; n. 꽥 하는 소리
If someone or something squeals, they make a long, high-pitched sound.

cross one's arms idiom 팔짱을 끼다
When you cross your arms, you put one of your arms over the other in front of your body, so that each hand is on the opposite elbow.

steal [stiːl] v. 훔치다, 도둑질하다; 살며시 움직이다
If you steal something from someone, you take it away from them without their permission and without intending to return it.

automatic [ɔ̀ːtəmǽtik] a. 무의식적인; 자동의 (**automatically** ad. 무의식적으로, 저절로)
An automatic action is one that you do without thinking about it.

tug [tʌg] v. (세게) 잡아당기다; n. (갑자기 세게) 잡아당김
If you tug something or tug at it, you give it a quick and usually strong pull.

dumb [dʌm] a. 멍청한, 바보 같은; 말을 못 하는
If you say that something is dumb, you think that it is silly and annoying.

attention [əténʃən] n. 주의, 주목; 관심, 흥미 (**pay attention** idiom 주의를 기울이다)
If you pay attention to someone, you watch them, listen to them, or take notice of them.

grouch [grauʧ] v. 불평하다; 토라지다; n. 불평; 불평꾼
To grouch means to complain a lot, often without good reason.

curious [kjúəriəs] a. 궁금한, 호기심이 많은; 별난, 특이한, 기이한
If you are curious about something, you are interested in it and want to know more about it.

lean [liːn] v. 기울이다, (몸을) 숙이다; ~에 기대다; a. 호리호리한
When you lean in a particular direction, you bend your body in that direction.

tap [tæp] v. (가볍게) 톡톡 두드리다; n. (가볍게) 두드리기
If you tap something, you hit it with a quick light blow or a series of quick light blows.

ankle [ǽŋkl] n. 발목
Your ankle is the joint where your foot joins your leg.

by oneself idiom 혼자; 도움을 받지 않고
If you are by yourselves, or all by yourselves, you are alone.

snack [snæk] n. 간식; v. 간식을 먹다

A snack is something such as a chocolate bar that you eat between meals.

ride [raid] v. (말·차량 등을) 타다; n. (말·차량 등을) 타고 달리기

When you ride a vehicle such as a car, you travel in it, especially as a passenger.

positive [pázətiv] a. 확신하는; 긍정적인; 분명한

If you are positive about something, you are completely sure about it.

poke [pouk] v. (손가락 등으로) 쿡 찌르다; 쑥 내밀다; n. (손가락 등으로) 찌르기

If you poke someone or something, you quickly push them with your finger or with a sharp object.

jiggle [dʒigl] v. (아래위·양옆으로 빠르게) 흔들다, 움직이다

If you jiggle something, you move it quickly up and down or from side to side.

sore [sɔːr] a. 아픈, 화끈거리는; 화가 난, 감정이 상한

If part of your body is sore, it causes you pain and discomfort.

throat [θrout] n. 목구멍; 목 (sore throat n. 인후염)

Your throat is the back of your mouth and the top part of the tubes that go down into your stomach and your lungs.

upset [ʌpsét] a. 속상한, 마음이 상한; v. 속상하게 하다

If you are upset, you are unhappy or disappointed because something unpleasant has happened to you.

spin [spin] v. (spun-spun) 돌아서다; (빙빙) 돌다; n. 회전

If you spin around, you turn your head or body quickly so that it faces the opposite direction.

regular [régjulər] a. 일반적인, 평범한; 규칙적인; n. 단골손님, 고정 고객

Regular is used to mean 'normal.'

ᵇ roll [roul] v. 구르다, 굴러가다; 굴리다; n. (둥글게 말아 놓은) 통, 두루마리
If you are lying down and you roll over, you turn your body so that a different part of you is facing upward.

⋆ stare [stɛər] v. 빤히 쳐다보다, 응시하다; n. 빤히 쳐다보기, 응시
If you stare at someone or something, you look at them for a long time.

ᵇ personal [pə́rsənl] a. 개인적인, 개인의
A personal relationship is one that is not connected with your job or public life.

ᵇ eyebrow [áibràu] n. 눈썹
Your eyebrows are the lines of hair which grow above your eyes.

leash [liːʃ] n. 가죽끈; 통제; v. 가죽끈으로 매다; 속박하다, 억제하다
A dog's leash is a long thin piece of leather or a chain, which you attach to the dog's collar so that you can keep the dog under control.

⋆ tackle [tǽkl] v. 달려들다; (힘든 문제·상황과) 씨름하다; n. (축구에서의) 태클
If you tackle someone, you attack them and fight them.

⋆ security [sikjúərəti] n. 경비 담당 부서; 보안, 경비; 안도감, 안심
Security means the department of a company or organization that deals with the protection of its buildings and equipment.

⋆ suspicious [səspíʃəs] a. 의심스러워하는; 의심스러운; 의혹을 갖는
If you are suspicious of someone or something, you do not trust them, and are careful when dealing with them.

jazz up idiom 더 신나게 하다; (음악을) 더 재즈처럼 만들다
If you jazz something up, you make it look more interesting, colorful, or exciting.

Chapter
4

1. What did Junie B. do at home?

A. She ate only a little bit of her sugar cereal.

B. She threw all of her sugar cereal in the trash.

C. She gave grown-up cereal to her dog.

D. She chose a grown-up cereal for breakfast.

2. Why did Junie B. become so happy on the bus?

A. Warren was not there.

B. The bus ride was short.

C. The fiber cereal helped her.

D. Grace's new shoes looked cool.

3. Why was Warren impressed by Grace?

A. She was really good at racing.

B. She was almost as fast as he was.

C. She had lightning stripes on her shoes.

D. She had been to the Olympics.

4. Why was Warren impressed by Lucille?

A. She had over a hundred dresses.

B. She looked like a princess.

C. Her family was famous.

D. Her family had a lot of money.

5. What did Junie B. try to do?

A. Show Warren that she was funny

B. Show Warren that she was normal

C. Show Warren that she was important

D. Show Warren that she was powerful

Check Your Reading Speed

1분에 몇 단어를 읽는지 리딩 속도를 측정해 보세요.

$$\frac{1,017 \text{ words}}{\text{reading time } (\quad) \text{ sec}} \times 60 = (\qquad) \text{ wPM}$$

Build Your Vocabulary

★ **stuff** [stʌf] n. 것, 물건, 일; v. 채워 넣다; 쑤셔 넣다
You can use stuff to refer to things such as a substance, a collection of things, events, or ideas, or the contents of something in a general way without mentioning the thing itself by name.

throw up idiom 토하다
If you throw up or throw something up, food and drink comes back up from your stomach and out of your mouth.

★ **rug** [rʌg] n. (작은 카펫같이 생긴) 깔개
A rug is a piece of thick material that you put on a floor.

★ **scream** [skriːm] v. 비명을 지르다, 괴성을 지르다; n. 비명, 절규
When someone screams, they make a very loud, high-pitched cry, because they are in pain or are very frightened.

‡ **sink** [siŋk] n. (부엌의) 개수대; 세면대; v. 가라앉다, 빠지다; 파다
A sink is a large fixed container in a kitchen or bathroom, with faucets to supply water.

‡ **handle** [hændl] v. (사람·작업 등을) 처리하다; 들다, 옮기다; n. 손잡이
If you say that someone can handle a problem or situation, you mean that they have the ability to deal with it successfully.

‡ **professional** [prəféʃənl] a. 전문적인; 능숙한; 직업상 적합한; n. 전문가
If you describe someone as professional, you mean that they are behaving in a correct way at work and doing your job well.

speedy [spíːdi] a. 빠른, 신속한
A speedy process, event, or action happens or is done very quickly.

grown-up [gróun-ʌp] a. 어른에게 맞는; n. 어른, 성인
Grown-up things seem suitable for or typical of adults.

jazz up idiom 더 신나게 하다; (음악을) 더 재즈처럼 만들다
If you jazz something up, you make it look more interesting, colorful, or exciting.

chew [ʧuː] v. (음식을) 씹다; 물어뜯다, 깨물다; n. 깨물기, 씹기
When you chew food, you use your teeth to break it up in your mouth so that it becomes easier to swallow.

grind [graind] v. (곡식 등을 잘게) 갈다; 문지르다; n. (기계의) 삐걱거리는 소리
If you grind a substance such as corn, you crush it between two hard surfaces or with a machine until it becomes a fine powder.

entire [intáiər] a. 전체의, 완전한, 온전한
You use entire when you want to emphasize that you are referring to the whole of something, for example, the whole of a place, time, or population.

lightning [láitniŋ] n. 번개, 번갯불; a. 아주 빠른; 급작스러운
Lightning is the very bright flashes of light in the sky that happen during thunderstorms.

stripe [straip] n. 줄무늬; v. 줄무늬를 넣다
A stripe is a long line which is a different color from the areas next to it.

discuss [diskʌ́s] v. 의견을 나누다, 논의하다; (말·글 등으로) 논하다
If people discuss something, they talk about it, often in order to reach a decision.

stuck [stʌk] a. 움직일 수 없는, 꼼짝 못하는; 갇힌
If something is stuck in a particular position, it is fixed tightly in this position and is unable to move.

poke [pouk] v. (손가락 등으로) 쿡 찌르다; 쑥 내밀다; n. (손가락 등으로) 찌르기
If you poke someone or something, you quickly push them with your finger or with a sharp object.

fingernail [fíŋgərnèil] n. 손톱
Your fingernails are the thin hard areas at the end of each of your fingers.

suck [sʌk] v. (입에 넣고) 빨아 먹다; (특정한 방향으로) 빨아들이다; n. 빨기, 빨아 먹기
If you suck something, you hold it in your mouth and pull at it with the muscles in your cheeks and tongue, for example in order to get liquid out of it.

smack [smæk] v. 탁 소리가 나게 치다; 세게 부딪치다; n. 강타; ad. 정통으로
(smack one's lips idiom 입맛을 다시다)
If you smack your lips, you open and close your mouth noisily, especially before or after eating, to show that you are eager to eat or enjoyed eating.

lip [lip] n. 입술; 테두리
Your lips are the two outer parts of the edge of your mouth.

lean [liːn] v. 기울이다, (몸을) 숙이다; ~에 기대다; a. 호리호리한
When you lean in a particular direction, you bend your body in that direction.

all of a sudden idiom 갑자기
If something happens all of a sudden, it happens quickly and unexpectedly.

clap [klæp] v. 박수를 치다; (갑자기·재빨리) 놓다; n. 박수; 쿵 하는 소리
When you clap, you hit your hands together to show appreciation or attract attention.

joyful [dʒɔ́ifəl] a. 아주 기뻐하는; 기쁜
Someone who is joyful is extremely happy.

calm [kaːm] a. 침착한, 차분한; 잔잔한; v. 진정시키다; 차분해지다
A calm person does not show or feel any worry, anger, or excitement.

‡‡still [stil] a. 가만히 있는, 고요한, 정지한; ad. 아직; 그럼에도 불구하고; v. 고요해지다
If you stay still, you stay in the same position and do not move.

‡hug [hʌg] v. 껴안다, 포옹하다; n. 포옹
When you hug someone, you put your arms around them and hold them tightly, for example because you like them or are pleased to see them.

‡bend [bend] v. (bent-bent) (몸·머리를) 굽히다, 숙이다; 구부리다; n. (도로·강의) 굽은 곳
When you bend, you move the top part of your body downward and forward.

٭dust [dʌst] v. 먼지를 털다; (고운 가루를) 뿌리다; n. 먼지, 티끌
When you dust something such as furniture, you remove dust from it, usually using a cloth.

huffy [hʌ́fi] a. 발끈 성내는, 홱 토라진
Someone who is huffy is obviously annoyed or offended about something.

‡breathe [briːð] v. 호흡하다, 숨을 쉬다
When people or animals breathe, they take air into their lungs and let it out again.

‡‡thrill [θril] v. 열광시키다, 정말 신나게 하다; n. 흥분, 설렘; 전율 (thrilled a. 아주 신이 난)
If someone is thrilled, they are extremely pleased about something.

‡‡water fountain [wɔ́ːtər fàuntən] n. (분수식) 식수대
A water fountain is a machine in a park or other public place that provides drinking water when you push a button.

perky [pə́ːrki] a. 활기찬, 생기 넘치는
If someone is perky, they are cheerful and lively.

zoom [zuːm] v. 쌩 하고 가다; 급등하다; n. (빠르게) 쌩 하고 지나가는 소리
If you zoom somewhere, you go there very quickly.

‡‡speed [spiːd] v. 빨리 가다; 더 빠르게 하다; 속도위반하다; n. 속도
If you speed somewhere, you move or travel there quickly, usually in a vehicle.

✲ bullet [búlit] n. 총알
A bullet is a small piece of metal with a pointed or rounded end, which is fired out of a gun.

✴ playground [pléigràund] n. (학교의) 운동장; 놀이터
A playground is a piece of land, at school or in a public area, where children can play.

✲ yell [jel] v. 고함치다, 소리 지르다; n. 고함, 외침
If you yell, you shout loudly, usually because you are excited, angry, or in pain.

✲ race [reis] n. 경주; 인종, 종족; v. 경주하다; 쏜살같이 가다; (머리·심장 등이) 바쁘게 돌아가다
A race is a competition to see who is the fastest, for example in running, swimming, or driving.

✴ bet [bet] v. (~이) 틀림없다; (내기 등에) 돈을 걸다; n. 짐작, 추측; 내기
If you say you bet that something is true or will happen, you mean you are certain that it is true or will happen.

✲ beat [bi:t] v. 이기다; 때리다; (심장이) 고동치다; n. 리듬; 고동, 맥박
If you beat someone in a competition or election, you defeat or do better than them.

pooped [pu:pt] a. 녹초가 된, 기진맥진한
If you are pooped, you are very tired.

✲ pop [pap] v. 불쑥 나타나다; 눈이 휘둥그레지다; 펑 하는 소리가 나다; n. 펑 (하는 소리)
If something pops, it suddenly appears, especially when not expected.

out of nowhere idiom 어디선지 모르게, 난데없이
If you say that something or someone appears out of nowhere, you mean that they appear suddenly and unexpectedly.

✲ spin [spin] v. (spun-spun) (빙빙) 돌다; 돌아서다; n. 회전
If something spins or if you spin it, it turns quickly around a central point.

✶ royal [rɔ́iəl] a. 국왕의; 성대한, 장엄한
Royal is used to indicate that something is connected with a king, queen, or emperor, or their family.

highness [háinis] n. 전하 (royal highness n. 전하)
Expressions such as 'Your Royal Highness' and 'Their Royal Highnesses' are used to address or refer to members of royal families who are not kings or queens.

복습 twirl [twəːrl] v. 빙글빙글 돌다, 빙글빙글 돌리다; 빙빙 돌리다; n. 회전
If you twirl, you turn around and around quickly, for example when you are dancing.

복습 include [inklúːd] v. 포함하다; ~을 (~에) 포함시키다
If one thing includes another thing, it has the other thing as one of its parts.

복습 tax [tæks] n. 세금; v. 세금을 부과하다, 과세하다
Tax is an amount of money that you have to pay to the government so that it can pay for public services.

복습 fluff [flʌf] v. 부풀리다; n. (동물이나 새의) 솜털; 보풀
If you fluff something, you shake or brush it so that it looks larger and softer.

✶ pleasant [plézənt] a. 상냥한, 예의 바른; 즐거운, 기분 좋은
A pleasant person is friendly and polite.

복습 plop [plap] v. 털썩 주저앉다; 떨어뜨리다; 풍덩 하고 떨어지다; n. 풍당 (하는 소리)
If someone plops or you plop them, they sit down or land heavily or without taking care.

복습 that's all idiom 그게 다이다, 그뿐이다
You can say 'that's all' at the end of a sentence when you say that there is nothing more involved than what you have mentioned.

✶✶ sign [sain] n. 몸짓, 신호; 표지판, 간판; 징후, 조짐; v. 서명하다; 신호를 보내다
A sign is a movement of your arms, hands, or head which is intended to have a particular meaning.

^{복습}**swing** [swiŋ] n. 그네; 흔들기; v. (전후·좌우로) 흔들다, 흔들리다; 휙 움직이다; 휘두르다

A swing is a seat hanging by two ropes or chains from a metal frame or from the branch of a tree.

Chapter
5

1. Why did Junie B. want to go to the mall?

    A. To buy things to wear for Warren

    B. To buy a present for Warren

    C. To meet her friends at a store

    D. To make her friends jealous

2. What did Junie B. try to do to Ollie?

    A. Steal his sweater from him

    B. Get him ready for the mall

    C. Put a leash on him

    D. Make him take a nap

3. **What did Junie B.'s mom say about making friends?**
   A. It took a lot of effort.
   B. It was not always possible.
   C. It required looking beautiful.
   D. It involved being fun and kind.

4. **What did Junie B.'s mom want Junie B. to do?**
   A. Just be herself
   B. Be nice to her brother
   C. Finish her dinner
   D. Act like her friends

5. **Why did Junie B. get excited about the ribbon?**
   A. She had lost it a long time ago.
   B. She could give it to Warren at school.
   C. It could help her look like a princess.
   D. It looked perfect on the teddy bear.

Check Your Reading Speed

1분에 몇 단어를 읽는지 리딩 속도를 측정해 보세요.

$$\frac{778 \text{ words}}{\text{reading time ( ) sec}} \times 60 = (\quad) \text{ wPM}$$

Build Your Vocabulary

복습 **hurray** [həréi] int. 만세

People sometimes shout 'Hurray!' when they are very happy and excited about something.

복습 **stuff** [stʌf] v. 쑤셔 넣다; 채워 넣다; n. 것, 물건, 일

If you stuff something somewhere, you push it there quickly and roughly.

복습 **make a face** idiom 얼굴을 찌푸리다, 침울한 표정을 짓다

If you make a face, you show a feeling such as dislike or disgust by putting an exaggerated expression on your face.

복습 **lightning** [láitniŋ] n. 번개, 번갯불; a. 아주 빠른; 급작스러운

Lightning is the very bright flashes of light in the sky that happen during thunderstorms.

★ **wipe** [waip] v. (먼지·물기 등을) 닦다; 지우다; n. 닦기

If you wipe dirt or liquid from something, you remove it, for example by using a cloth or your hand.

fill up idiom 배를 가득 채우다, 배가 부르다

If you fill up or fill yourself up with food, you eat so much that you do not feel hungry.

★★ **hall** [hɔːl] n. (건물 내의) 복도, 통로; (크고 넓은) 방, 홀, 회관

A hall in a building is a long passage with doors into rooms on both sides of it.

zoom [zu:m] v. 쌩 하고 가다; 급등하다; n. (빠르게) 쌩 하고 지나가는 소리
If you zoom somewhere, you go there very quickly.

nursery [nə́:rsəri] n. 아기 방; 탁아소, 유치원
A nursery is a room in a family home in which the young children of the family sleep or play.

holler [hálər] v. 소리 지르다, 고함치다; n. 고함, 외침
If you holler, you shout loudly.

crib [krib] n. 아기 침대; 구유, 여물통
A crib is a bed for a small baby.

giant [dʒáiənt] a. 거대한, 엄청나게 큰; 비범한; n. 거인
Something that is described as giant is extremely large, strong, powerful, or important.

fit [fit] v. (모양·크기가) 맞다; 적절하다; 어울리게 하다; a. 적합한, 알맞은; 건강한
If something fits, it is the right size and shape to go onto a person's body or onto a particular object.

nap [næp] n. 낮잠, 잠깐 잠; v. 잠깐 자다, 낮잠을 자다
If you have a nap, you have a short sleep, usually during the day.

pat [pæt] v. 쓰다듬다, 토닥거리다; n. 쓰다듬기, 토닥거리기
If you pat something or someone, you tap them lightly, usually with your hand held flat.

leash [li:ʃ] n. 가죽끈; 통제; v. 가죽끈으로 매다; 속박하다, 억제하다
A dog's leash is a long thin piece of leather or a chain, which you attach to the dog's collar so that you can keep the dog under control.

jazz up idiom 더 신나게 하다; (음악을) 더 재즈처럼 만들다
If you jazz something up, you make it look more interesting, colorful, or exciting.

control [kəntróul] v. 통제하다; 지배하다; 조정하다; n. 통제, 제어; 지배
If you control someone or something, you make them do what you want, or make something happen in the way that you want.

roll one's eyes idiom 눈을 굴리다
If you roll your eyes or if your eyes roll, they move round and upward to show you are bored or annoyed.

stamp [stæmp] v. (발을) 구르다; 쾅쾅거리며 걷다; (도장 등을) 찍다; n. (발을) 쿵쾅거리기; 도장
If you stamp or stamp your foot, you lift your foot and put it down very hard on the ground, for example because you are angry.

careful [kέərfəl] a. 신중한, 조심하는; 주의 깊은; 세심한 (carefully ad. 주의하여)
If you are careful, you give serious attention to what you are doing, in order to avoid harm, damage, or mistakes.

lift [lift] v. 들어 올리다, 올라가다; n. (차 등을) 태워 주기
If you lift something, you move it to another position, especially upward.

honest [ánist] a. 정직한; 솔직한; ad. 정말로, 틀림없이 (honesty n. 정직, 솔직)
If you describe someone as honest, you mean that they always tell the truth, and do not try to deceive people or break the law.

pretend [priténd] v. ~인 척하다, ~인 것처럼 굴다; ~라고 가장하다
If you pretend that something is the case, you act in a way that is intended to make people believe that it is the case, although in fact it is not.

smooth [smu:ð] v. 매끈하게 하다, 반듯하게 펴다; a. 매끈한; 부드러운; (소리가) 감미로운
If you smooth something, you move your hands over its surface to make it smooth and flat.

sniffle [snifl] n. 훌쩍거림; 훌쩍거리는 소리; v. (계속) 훌쩍거리다
A sniffle is an act or sound of breathing in quickly and repeatedly through the nose, for example because you are crying or you have a cold.

snort [snɔ:rt] n. 코웃음, 콧방귀; (말이) 코를 힝힝거리는 소리;
v. (말이) 코를 힝힝거리다; 코웃음을 치다, 콧방귀를 뀌다
A snort is a sudden loud noise that you make through your nose, for example because you are angry or laughing.

swallow [swálou] n. (음식 등을) 삼키기; [동물] 제비; v. 삼키다; 마른침을 삼키다
A swallow is an action in which you make food or drink go from your mouth down into your stomach.

^복^습 **think over** idiom ~을 심사숙고하다
If you think something over, you consider it carefully, especially before making a decision.

^복^습 **shoulder** [ʃóuldər] n. 어깨; (옷의) 어깨 부분
Your shoulder is one of the two parts of your body between your neck and the top of your arms.

^복^습 **shelf** [ʃelf] n. 선반; 책꽂이, (책장의) 칸
A shelf is a flat piece of wood, metal, or glass which is attached to a wall or to the sides of a cupboard, used for keeping things on.

^복^습 **exact** [igzǽkt] a. 정확한; 꼼꼼한, 빈틈없는 (exactly ad. 정확히, 꼭)
You use exactly before an amount, number, or position to emphasize that it is no more, no less, or no different from what you are stating.

^복^습 **bow** [bou] ① n. 나비매듭 리본; 활 ② n. (고개 숙여 하는) 인사; 절; v. (허리를 굽혀) 절하다
A bow is a knot with two loops and two loose ends that is used in tying shoelaces and ribbons.

_★ **gorgeous** [gɔ́:rdʒəs] a. 아주 멋진, 아름다운; 선명한, 화려한
If you say that something is gorgeous, you mean that it gives you a lot of pleasure or is very attractive.

^복^습 **sparkly** [spá:rkli] a. 활기 있는, 생기에 찬; 반짝반짝 빛나는
If you describe someone as sparkly, you mean that they are lively and witty.

Chapter
6

1. How did Junie B. feel about her princess outfit?

A. She was glad to have brand-new princess things.

B. She was proud to wear many princess things.

C. She was worried that her princess things looked silly.

D. She was embarrassed that her princess things were not real.

2. What did Grace do on the bus?

A. She tried on Junie B.'s crown.

B. She said that Junie B. looked terrible.

C. She stopped speaking to Junie B.

D. She would not sit with Junie B.

3. How did Warren react to Junie B.'s clothes?

A. He did not look at them.

B. He was confused by them.

C. He thought that they were strange.

D. He believed that they were princess clothes.

4. Why did Warren yell at the girls?

A. He did not want them to leave.

B. He did not want to be around them.

C. He wanted more attention from them.

D. He wanted them to stop fighting.

5. How did Lucille and Grace respond?

A. They asked Warren what was wrong.

B. They comforted Warren because he was sad.

C. They told Warren that he was their friend.

D. They got mad at Warren for being mean.

Check Your Reading Speed

1분에 몇 단어를 읽는지 리딩 속도를 측정해 보세요.

$$\frac{649 \text{ words}}{\text{reading time ( ) sec}} \times 60 = (\quad) \text{ wPM}$$

Build Your Vocabulary

speechless [spíːʧlis] a. (충격 등으로) 말을 못 하는
If you are speechless, you are temporarily unable to speak, usually because something has shocked you.

all the way idiom 완전히; 내내, 시종
If you do something all the way, you do it totally and completely.

gorgeous [gɔ́ːrdʒəs] a. 아주 멋진, 아름다운; 선명한, 화려한
If you say that something is gorgeous, you mean that it gives you a lot of pleasure or is very attractive.

fluff [flʌf] v. 부풀리다; n. (동물이나 새의) 솜털; 보풀
If you fluff something, you shake or brush it so that it looks larger and softer.

collar [kálər] n. (개 등의) 목걸이; (윗옷의) 칼라, 깃
A collar is a band of leather or plastic which is put around the neck of a dog or cat.

silly [síli] a. 어리석은, 바보 같은; 우스꽝스러운; n. 바보
If you say that someone or something is silly, you mean that they are foolish, childish, or ridiculous.

lovely [lʌ́vli] a. 훌륭한, 멋진; 사랑스러운, 아름다운
If you describe someone or something as lovely, you mean that they are very beautiful and therefore pleasing to look at or listen to.

* jewel [dʒúːəl] n. 보석; 귀중품
A jewel is a precious stone used to decorate valuable things that you wear, such as rings or necklaces.

* notice [nóutis] v. 알아채다, 인지하다; 주의하다; n. 신경 씀, 주목, 알아챔
If you notice something or someone, you become aware of them.

* golden [góuldən] a. 황금빛의; 금으로 만든; 특별한, 소중한
Something that is golden is bright yellow in color.

* crown [kraun] n. 왕관; 왕권; v. 왕관을 씌우다, 왕위에 앉히다
A crown is a circular ornament, usually made of gold and jewels, which a king or queen wears on their head at official ceremonies.

복습 bow [bou] ① n. 나비매듭 리본; 활 ② n. (고개 숙여 하는) 인사; 절; v. (허리를 굽혀) 절하다
A bow is a knot with two loops and two loose ends that is used in tying shoelaces and ribbons.

복습 lightning [láitniŋ] n. 번개, 번갯불; a. 아주 빠른; 급작스러운
Lightning is the very bright flashes of light in the sky that happen during thunderstorms.

복습 twirl [twəːrl] v. 빙글빙글 돌다, 빙글빙글 돌리다; 빙빙 돌리다; n. 회전
If you twirl, you turn around and around quickly, for example when you are dancing.

get a load of idiom (자세히) 보다, (주의해서) 듣다
People sometimes say 'Get a load of that!' to tell someone to pay attention to a person or thing that is interesting, surprising, or attractive.

slump [slʌmp] v. 털썩 앉다; 푹 쓰러지다; (가치·수량 등이) 급감하다; n. 부진; 불황
If you slump somewhere, you fall or sit down there heavily, for example because you are very tired or you feel ill.

복습 race [reis] v. 쏜살같이 가다; 경주하다; (머리·심장 등이) 바쁘게 돌아가다; n. 경주; 인종, 종족
If you race somewhere, you go there as quickly as possible.

scratch [skrætʃ] v. 긁다; 긁힌 자국을 내다; n. 긁힌 자국; 긁는 소리
If a sharp object scratches someone or something, it makes small shallow cuts on their skin or surface.

knee [niː] n. 무릎; v. 무릎으로 치다
Your knee is the place where your leg bends.

tap [tæp] v. (가볍게) 톡톡 두드리다; n. (가볍게) 두드리기
If you tap something, you hit it with a quick light blow or a series of quick light blows.

sight [sait] n. 구경거리; 광경, 모습; 시력; 시야; v. 갑자기 보다
A sight can refer to a person or place that is very unusual, untidy, or unpleasant to look at.

roll one's eyes idiom 눈을 굴리다
If you roll your eyes or if your eyes roll, they move round and upward to show you are bored or annoyed.

do good idiom (~에게) 도움이 되다, 이롭다
If you say that something will do someone good, you mean that it will benefit them or improve them.

squat [skwat] v. 쪼그리고 앉다, 웅크리다; a. 땅딸막한; 쪼그리고 앉은
If you squat, you lower yourself toward the ground, balancing on your feet with your legs bent.

stare [stɛər] v. 빤히 쳐다보다, 응시하다; n. 빤히 쳐다보기, 응시
If you stare at someone or something, you look at them for a long time.

patient [péiʃənt] a. 참을성 있는, 인내심 있는; n. 환자
If you are patient, you stay calm and do not get annoyed, for example, when something takes a long time, or when someone is not doing what you want them to do.

lean [liːn] v. 기울이다, (몸을) 숙이다; ~에 기대다; a. 호리호리한
When you lean in a particular direction, you bend your body in that direction.

^복_습 **all of a sudden** idiom 갑자기
If something happens all of a sudden, it happens quickly and unexpectedly.

^복_습 **handle** [hǽndl] v. (사람·작업 등을) 처리하다; 들다, 옮기다; n. 손잡이
If you say that someone can handle a problem or situation, you mean that they have the ability to deal with it successfully.

^복_습 **huffy** [hʌ́fi] a. 발끈 성내는, 홱 토라진
Someone who is huffy is obviously annoyed or offended about something.

^복_습 **stomp** [stamp] v. 쿵쿵거리며 걷다; 발을 구르며 춤추다
If you stomp somewhere, you walk there with very heavy steps, often because you are angry.

⋆ **furious** [fjúəriəs] a. 몹시 화가 난; 맹렬한
Someone who is furious is extremely angry.

eyeball [áibɔl] n. 안구, 눈알; v. (무례할 정도로) 눈을 동그랗게 뜨고 쳐다보다
Your eyeballs are your whole eyes, rather than just the part which can be seen between your eyelids.

^복_습 **bend** [bend] v. (bent-bent) (몸·머리를) 굽히다, 숙이다; 구부리다; n. (도로·강의) 굽은 곳
When you bend, you move the top part of your body downward and forward.

⋆ **groan** [groun] n. 신음, 끙 하는 소리; v. (고통·짜증으로) 신음 소리를 내다; 끙끙거리다
A groan is a long low sound that a person makes, especially when they are in pain or unhappy.

Chapter
7

1. Why did Junie B. continue to bother Warren?

    A. She could not find Grace and Lucille.

    B. She wanted him to like her clothes.

    C. She was trying to annoy him.

    D. She saw something stuck in his hair.

2. Why was Warren upset?

    A. He missed his old school.

    B. He was going to move soon.

    C. His friends were angry at him.

    D. His dad did not like their new home.

3. Why did Junie B. start telling jokes?

    A. She wanted to teach them to Warren.

    B. She wanted to prove that she was funny.

    C. She wanted to cheer Warren up.

    D. She wanted to stop being bored.

4. What did Warren finally do?

    A. He asked Junie B. to tell more jokes.

    B. He felt better and told a joke.

    C. He laughed because he really sneezed.

    D. He talked about Junie B.'s princess clothes.

5. How were Junie B. and Warren nutballs?

    A. They had no other friends.

    B. They were laughing on the ground.

    C. They were telling jokes wrong.

    D. They knew so many jokes.

Check Your Reading Speed
1분에 몇 단어를 읽는지 리딩 속도를 측정해 보세요.

$$\frac{980 \ words}{reading \ time \ (\quad) \ sec} \times 60 = (\quad) \ wPM$$

Build Your Vocabulary

✻ **knock** [nak] n. 문 두드리는 소리; 부딪침; v. (문 등을) 두드리다; 치다, 부딪치다
A knock is the sound of someone hitting a door or window with their hand or with something hard to attract attention.

⁎ **bother** [báðər] v. 귀찮게 하다, 귀찮게 말을 걸다; 신경 쓰이게 하다; 신경 쓰다; n. 성가심
If someone bothers you, they talk to you when you want to be left alone or interrupt you when you are busy.

복습 **personal** [pə́rsənl] a. 개인적인, 개인의
A personal opinion, quality, or thing belongs or relates to one particular person rather than to other people.

복습 **that's all** idiom 그게 다이다, 그뿐이다
You can say 'that's all' at the end of a sentence when you say that there is nothing more involved than what you have mentioned.

복습 **teeny** [tíːni] a. 아주 작은
If you describe something as teeny, you are emphasizing that it is very small.

✻ **brush** [brʌʃ] v. (솔이나 손으로) 털다; 솔질을 하다; (붓을 이용하여) 바르다; n. 붓; 솔
If you brush something somewhere, you remove it with quick light movements of your hands.

patient [péiʃənt] a. 참을성 있는, 인내심 있는; n. 환자
If you are patient, you stay calm and do not get annoyed, for example, when something takes a long time, or when someone is not doing what you want them to do.

tap [tæp] v. (가볍게) 톡톡 두드리다; n. (가볍게) 두드리기
If you tap something, you hit it with a quick light blow or a series of quick light blows.

blow [blou] v. (blew-blown) (입으로) 불다; (바람·입김에) 날리다; 폭파하다; n. 강타
(blow one's nose idiom 코를 풀다)
When you blow your nose, you force air out of it through your nostrils in order to clear it.

stuck [stʌk] a. 움직일 수 없는, 꼼짝 못하는; 갇힌
If something is stuck in a particular position, it is fixed tightly in this position and is unable to move.

pleasant [plézənt] a. 즐거운, 기분 좋은; 상냥한, 예의 바른
Something that is pleasant is nice, enjoyable, or attractive.

all of a sudden idiom 갑자기
If something happens all of a sudden, it happens quickly and unexpectedly.

cover [kʌ́vər] v. 가리다; 덮다; n. 덮개; (pl.) (침대) 커버, 이불 (uncover v. 덮개를 벗기다)
To uncover something means to remove something that is covering it.

holler [hálər] v. 소리 지르다, 고함치다; n. 고함, 외침
If you holler, you shout loudly.

period [píːəriəd] int. 끝, 이상이다; n. 기간, 시기; 시대; 끝
You can say 'period' at the end of a statement to show that you believe you have said all there is to say on a subject and you are not going to discuss it any more.

roll one's eyes idiom 눈을 굴리다
If you roll your eyes or if your eyes roll, they move round and upward to show you are bored or annoyed.

handle [hændl] v. (사람·작업 등을) 처리하다; 들다, 옮기다; n. 손잡이
If you say that someone can handle a problem or situation, you mean that they have the ability to deal with it successfully.

yell [jel] v. 고함치다, 소리 지르다; n. 고함, 외침
If you yell, you shout loudly, usually because you are excited, angry, or in pain.

on account of idiom ~때문에
You use on account of to introduce the reason or explanation for something.

grouchy [gráuʧi] a. 시무룩해진; 불평이 많은, 잘 투덜거리는
If someone is grouchy, they are very bad-tempered and complain a lot.

knee [niː] n. 무릎; v. 무릎으로 치다
Your knee is the place where your leg bends.

sniffle [snifl] v. (계속) 훌쩍거리다; n. 훌쩍거림; 훌쩍거리는 소리
If you sniffle, you keep breathing in noisily through your nose, for example because you are crying or you have a cold.

pat [pæt] v. 쓰다듬다, 토닥거리다; n. 쓰다듬기, 토닥거리기
If you pat something or someone, you tap them lightly, usually with your hand held flat.

pop [pap] v. 불쑥 나타나다; 눈이 휘둥그레지다; 펑 하는 소리가 나다; n. 펑 (하는 소리)
If something pops, it suddenly appears, especially when not expected.

★ **tickle** [tikl] v. 간지럼을 태우다; 간질간질하다; 재미있게 하다; n. (장난으로) 간지럽히기
When you tickle someone, you move your fingers lightly over a sensitive part of their body, often in order to make them laugh.

give it a try idiom 시도하다, 한번 해 보다
If you decide to give an activity a try, you do it even though it is something that you have never tried before.

^복_습 **jiggle** [dʒígl] v. (아래위·양옆으로 빠르게) 흔들다, 움직이다
If you jiggle something, you move it quickly up and down or from side to side.

^복_습 **golden** [góuldən] a. 황금빛의; 금으로 만든; 특별한, 소중한
Something that is golden is bright yellow in color.

^복_습 **crown** [kraun] n. 왕관; 왕권; v. 왕관을 씌우다, 왕위에 앉히다
A crown is a circular ornament, usually made of gold and jewels, which a king or queen wears on their head at official ceremonies.

^복_습 **million** [míljən] n. 100만; a. 100만의; 수많은 (like a million bucks idiom 아주 좋은)
If you look or feel like a million bucks, you look or feel extremely good, often because you are wearing something that costs a lot of money.

^복_습 **collar** [kálər] n. (개 등의) 목걸이; (윗옷의) 칼라, 깃
A collar is a band of leather or plastic which is put around the neck of a dog or cat.

^복_습 **still** [stil] a. 가만히 있는, 고요한, 정지한; ad. 아직; 그럼에도 불구하고; v. 고요해지다
If you stay still, you stay in the same position and do not move.

_* **sigh** [sai] n. 한숨; v. 한숨을 쉬다, 한숨짓다; 탄식하듯 말하다
A sigh is a slow breath out that makes a long soft sound, especially because you are disappointed, tired, annoyed, or relaxed.

^복_습 **grouch** [grautʃ] v. 불평하다; 토라지다; n. 불평; 불평꾼
To grouch means to complain a lot, often without good reason.

_* **sneeze** [sni:z] v. 재채기하다; n. 재채기
When you sneeze, you suddenly take in your breath and then blow it down your nose noisily without being able to stop yourself, for example because you have a cold.

^복_습 **peek** [pi:k] v. 살짝 보이다; (재빨리) 훔쳐보다; n. 엿보기
If someone or something peeks, they appear slightly from behind or under something.

fist [fist] n. 주먹
Your hand is referred to as your fist when you have bent your fingers in toward the palm in order to hit someone, to make an angry gesture, or to hold something.

underpants [ʌ́ndərpænts] n. (pl.) (남성용·여성용) 팬티
Underpants are a piece of underwear covering the area between the waist and the tops of the legs.

clap [klæp] v. 박수를 치다; (갑자기·재빨리) 놓다; n. 박수; 쿵 하는 소리
When you clap, you hit your hands together to show appreciation or attract attention.

twirl [twəːrl] v. 빙글빙글 돌다, 빙글빙글 돌리다; 빙빙 돌리다; n. 회전
If you twirl, you turn around and around quickly, for example when you are dancing.

bouncy [báunsi] a. 잘 튀는, 탱탱한; 활기 넘치는
A bouncy thing can bounce very well or makes other things bounce well.

light [lait] v. (lit-lit) 밝아지다; 불을 붙이다; n. 빛
If a person's eyes or face light up, or something lights them up, they become bright with excitement or happiness.

side [said] n. (사람 몸통의) 옆구리; 옆; (한) 쪽
Your sides are the parts of your body between your front and your back, from under your arms to your hips.

roll [roul] v. 구르다, 굴러가다; 굴리다; n. (둥글게 말아 놓은) 통, 두루마리
If you are lying down and you roll over, you turn your body so that a different part of you is facing upward.

brand-new [brænd-njúː] a. 아주 새로운, 신상품의
A brand-new object is completely new.

1장 잘생긴 워런(Warren)

내 이름은 주니 B. 존스(Junie B. Jones)입니다. B는 비어트리스(Beatrice)를 나타냅니다. 하지만 나는 비어트리스라는 이름을 좋아하지 않습니다.

나는 그냥 B를 좋아할 뿐이고 그게 다입니다.

나는 학교 유치부에 다니는 학년입니다.

나의 교실은 9반(Room Nine)이라 불려요.

나는 그곳에 두 명의 가장 친한 친구가 있습니다.

그들 중 한 명의 이름은 루실(Lucille)입니다.

그녀는 나보다 훨씬 더 예쁩니다. 그것은 그녀의 할머니가 그녀에게 화려한 원피스를 사 주기 때문입니다. 그리고 또 그녀가 리본이 달린 레이스 양말도 가지고 있기 때문입니다.

내 다른 친구의 이름은 그레이스(Grace)입니다. 나와 그 그레이스는 함께 스쿨버스를 탑니다.

그녀는 내가 가장 좋아하는 종류의 머리카락을 가지고 있습니다. 그것은 자연 곱슬이라고 불립니다.

또, 그녀는 분홍색 하이 톱 운동화도 가지고 있습니다. 그리고 재빠른 발도요.

그 그레이스는 학교 유치부의 모든 아이들 중 가장 빠른 달리기 선수입니다.

그녀는 우리가 하는 모든 달리기 경주에서 나를 이기고는 해요.

나는 그것에 대해 잘 받아들이는 사람입니다. 하지만 가끔 나는 그녀를 반칙쟁이라는 이름으로 부릅니다.

나와 그 그레이스와 루실은 학교 시작 전에 함께 말처럼 뛰놉니다.

말처럼 뛰노는 것은 여러분이 질주하는 때입니다. 그리고 빨리 걷는 때이지요. 그리고 코로 히힝거리는 소리를 내는 시간을 말해요.

나는 밤톨이(Brownie)입니다. 루실은 까망이(Blackie)입니다. 그리고 그 그레이스는 노랑이(Yellowie)입니다.

하지만 오늘, 나와 그 그레이스는 어디에서도 루실을 찾을 수 없었습니다.

우리는 그녀를 찾아 사방을 모두 뒤졌습니다.

"이런." 내가 말했습니다. "이제 우리는 그렇게 잘 말처럼 놀 수는 없을 거야. 왜냐면('cause) 말이 두 마리일 때는 말이 세 마리일 때만큼 재미있지 않거든."

"어쩌면 루실이 그냥 늦는 건지도 몰라." 그 그레이스가 말했습니다. "아니면 혹시 걔네 집에 뭔가 문제가 생겼나 봐."

나는 아주 깊이 생각하며 내 턱을 톡톡 쳤습니다.

"그래." 내가 말했습니다. "어쩌면 루실의 할아버지가 걔네 집으로 앵무새 한 마리를 데려왔을지도 몰라. 그리고 루실은 학교에 가려고 옷을 입던 중이었지. 그리고 그때 그 앵무새가 루실의 방으로 날아들었던 거야. 그리고 앵무새는 루실의 머리카락에 완전히 뒤엉켜 버렸던 거지. 그리고 그래서 걔네 할아버지가 911에 전화를 걸어야 했던 거야. 그리고 진짜 실제 소방관이 루실의 집으로 온 거지. 그리고 소방관은 가위로 루실의 머리카락을 잘라 앵무새를 빼냈어. 하지만 그건 머리가 없는 작은 부분 하나를 남겼겠지. 그런데 이거 알아? 만약 네가 커다란 리본을 머리에 한다면, 아무도 그 차이를 알 수 없어."

그 그레이스는 내 커다란 리본을 의아하게 바라보았습니다.

나는 침을 꿀꺽 삼켰습니다.

"좋아, 그런데 내가 아예 그걸 너에게 말하지 않았던 걸로 해 줘." 내가 아주 부드럽게 말했습니다.

그 후, 나와 그 그레이스는 조금 더 루실을 찾아다녔습니다.

그리고 맞혀 볼래요?

내가 그녀를 발견했어요! 바로 그거죠!

"얘, 그레이스! 나 루실이 보여! 내가 루실을 봤다고! 걔 지금 식수대를 지나서 뛰어가고 있어!"

그 그레이스도 마찬가지로, 그녀를 발견했습니다.

"얘! 누군가가 루실을 뒤쫓고 있어, 주니 B.!" 그녀가 소리쳤습니다. "저 남자애는 누구지? 루실을 뒤쫓고 있는 저 남자애는 도대체 누구야?"

나는 내 눈을 정말 아주 가늘게 떴습니다.

"저건 사악한 낯선 남자애야, 그레이스!" 내가 대답하며 외쳤습니다. "사악하고 낯선 남자애가 루실을 뒤쫓고 있다고! 그리고 그래서 이제 너와 내가 루실을 구해 줘야 할 거야!"

나는 빠르게 원을 그리며 나의 팔을 흔들었습니다.

"서둘러, 노랑아! 가자! 루실을 구하러 가자!"

그런 다음 나와 그 그레이스는 즉시 행동했습니다!

우리는 그 낯선 남자아이를 쫓아 전속력으로 질주했습니다!

그 그레이스는 그를 아주 재빠르게 따라잡았습니다.

그녀는 자신의 팔을 이리저리 휘둘렀습니다.

"저리 가, 악당아! 저리 사라져서 루실을 가만히 내버려 두란 말이야!" 그녀가 고함쳤습니다.

"맞아!" 내가 외쳤습니다. "루실을 가만히 내버려 둬! 안 그러면 내가 널 교장 선생님에게 이를 거야! 왜냐면 나랑 교장 선생님은 개인적인 친구 사이니까. 그리고 교장 선생님은 네 머리를 마구 때릴 거야!"

그다음에도, 나와 그 그레이스는 그가 달아날 때까지 계속해서 우리의 팔을 휘둘렀습니다.

그리고 나서 우리는 하이 파이브를 했습니다.

"만세!" 우리는 외쳤습니다. "만세! 만세! 우리가 저 사악하고 낯선 남자애한테서 루실을 구했어!"

갑자기, 루실은 몹시 화가 나서 우리에게 발을 쿵쿵 구르며 다가왔습니다.

"너희들 왜 그런 짓을 했어?" 그녀가 소리 질렀습니다. "너희는 왜 그 남자애를 쫓아 버린 거야? 지금 너희들이 전부 망쳤다고!"

나와 그 그레이스는 놀라서 그녀를 바라보았습니다.

"하지만 우리는 네가 그렇게 해 주길 *바라는* 줄 알았어." 그 그레이스가 말했습니다.

"우린 너를 그 사악하고 낯선 남자애에게서 구해 줬는걸." 나는 정말 자랑스럽게 설명했습니다.

루실은 씩씩댔습니다.

"그 애는 사악하고 낯선 남자애가 아니야, 주니 B.! 걔는 8반(Room Eight)에 새로 온 아이야. 그리고 그 애 이름은 워런이야! 그리고 걘 내가 지금까지 본 사람 중 가장 잘생긴 남자애라고! 걔는 예전에 *TV* 광고에도 나온 적 있단 말이야!"

나와 그 그레이스는 눈썹을 치켜올렸습니다.

"걔가?" 그 그레이스가 말했습니다.

"걔가 예전에 TV 광고에 나온 적이 있다고?" 내가 말했습니다.

그 그레이스는 까치발로 섰습니다.

"그 애가 어디로 갔지? 난 걔를 자세히 보지도 못했어." 그녀가 말했습니다.

"나도." 내가 말했습니다. "나도 마찬가지로, 그 애를 자세히 보지 못했어. 걔가 얼마나 잘생긴 거야, 루실? 그 애 영화배우처럼 잘생겼니?"

바로 그때, 그 그레이스가 정말 신이 나서 폴짝폴짝 뛰었습니다.

"저기 그 남자애다! 걔 저기 있어! 그 애가 저기 저 나무 아래에 있다고! 그 애 보이니, 주니 B.? 쟤 보이지?"

나는 그 남자아이를 향해 내 눈을 할 수 있는 한 가장 가늘게 떴습니다.

그러자 머리에서 내 두 눈이 실제로 튀어나올 뻔했습니다!

왜냐면 그는 정말로 영화배우처럼 잘생겼기 때문이죠! 그래서 그렇습니다!

"우와-우와우-와우! 정말 엄청나잖

아!" 내가 말했습니다. "내 생각에, 나는 저 남자애가 나의 새 남자친구가 됐으면 좋겠어!"

루실은 나를 향해 매서운 눈빛을 보냈습니다.

"안 돼!" 그녀는 소리쳤습니다. "그렇게 말하지 마, 주니 B.! 그 애는 네 남자친구가 될 수 없어. 걔는 내 남자친구만 될 수 있다고. 왜냐면 내가 그 애를 먼저 봤으니까!"

나는 그 말을 아주 신중하게 생각했습니다.

"알겠어, 그런데 여기 문제가 있어, 루실." 내가 말했습니다. "나와 그 그레이스는 사실 그 애에게 아직 시도도 못해 봤잖아."

"그래." 그 그레이스가 말했습니다. "우린 분명 그 애랑 이야기해 볼 필요가 있어. 그리고 그래서 이제 네가 우리를 소개해 줘야겠어."

루실은 자신의 발을 굴렸습니다.

"안 돼!" 그녀가 외쳤습니다. "안 돼! 안 돼! 안 된다고! 왜냐면 너희들이 내게서 워런을 빼앗아 갈 거니까! 그리고 그건 심지어 공평하지도 않다고! 또, 주니 B.는 이미 남자친구가 있잖아. 기억하지, 주니 B.? 너에게는 이미 리카도 (Ricardo)가 있다고! 기억하지?"

나는 잘생긴 워런을 또 한 번 살짝 훔쳐보았습니다.

"응, 그렇지만 내 생각에 나는 아마 다른 사람을 만날 준비가 된 것 같아." 나는 아주 조용히 말했습니다.

바로 그때 루실의 얼굴에 분노가 가득찼습니다. 그리고 그녀는 쿵쾅거리며 아주 재빨리 우리를 떠났습니다.

하지만 나와 그 그레이스는 신경 쓰지도 않았습니다.

우리는 그저 계속해서 그 잘생긴 남자아이를 살짝 훔쳐보고 또 훔쳐봤습니다.

왜냐면 그는 우리 눈에 미남이었으니까요.

2장 돼지 같은 아이들

루실은 9반에서 내 옆에 앉습니다.

나는 계속해서 그녀에게 상냥하게 굴었습니다.

왜냐면 당연하게도, 나는 그 잘생긴 남자아이를 만나고 싶었기 때문입니다.

"다시 친구 할래, 루실? 응? 우리 예전에 그랬던 것처럼 친구가 되어 볼까? 그건 우리에게 좋을 것 같아, 그렇지 않니?"

"안 그래." 루실이 말했습니다. "넌 그냥 나의 새 남자친구를 뺏으려고 친구가 되고 싶다는 것뿐이잖아."

나는 그녀에게 크게 숨을 내쉬었습니다.

"좋아, 그런데 내가 어떻게 그 애를 뺏을 수나 있겠어, 루실?" 내가 물었습니다. "왜냐면 넌 나보다 훨씬 더 예쁘니까. 그거 알지? 네가 나보다 얼마나 더 예쁜지 기억하지?"

루실은 기억했습니다.

그녀는 한껏 우쭐거렸습니다.

그런 다음 그녀는 나에게 자신의 새로운 레이스 양말을 보여 주었습니다.

"8달러 50센트야. . . 세금은 빼고." 그녀가 말했습니다.

나는 양말을 보고 눈이 휘둥그레졌습니다.

"우와-우와우-와우. 당신은 정말 화려한 발을 가지고 있군요, 아가씨!" 내가 말했습니다.

그 후, 나도 마찬가지로, 루실에게 내 양말을 보여 주었습니다.

"보여, 루실? 내 양말 보여? 이건 아주 축 처지고 늘어졌지. 그건 어젯밤 나와 내 강아지 티클(Tickle)이 이것들로 줄다리기를 했기 때문이야. 그리고 티클은 양말에 침을 흘렸고."

루실은 얼굴을 찌푸렸습니다.

"웩." 그녀가 말했습니다.

"나도 이게 웩이란 걸 알지." 내가 대답했습니다. "이게 바로 내가 너한테 말하려던 거야, 루실. 나는 정말 돼지 같

은 아이라고. 그리고 그래서 어떻게 내가 네 남자친구를 뺏을 수나 있겠어?"

바로 그때, 루실은 나를 조금 더 상냥하게 바라보았습니다.

나는 서둘러 내 의자를 그녀에게 가까이 가져갔습니다.

"이제 우리는 다시 친구야! 맞지, 루실? 맞지?" 내가 말했습니다. "그리고 그러면 이제 너는 나를 잘생긴 워런에게 소개해 줄 수 있겠네. 왜냐면 난 그 남자애를 빼앗지도 않을 테니까."

루실은 조금 더 우쭐거렸습니다.

"난 잘 모르겠어. . . 내가 좀 더 생각해 볼게." 그녀가 말했습니다.

나는 정말 신이 나 손뼉을 쳤습니다.

그러고 나서 나는 빠르게 내 의자 위에 일어섰습니다.

"그레이스! 야, 그레이스!" 나는 소리쳤습니다. "루실이 자기가 좀 더 생각해 본대!"

바로 그때, 나는 다른 사람의 목소리를 들었습니다.

"주니 B. 존스! 너 도대체 뭐 하고 있는 거니?"

그것은 나의 선생님이었습니다.

그녀의 이름은 선생님(Mrs.)입니다.

마찬가지로, 그녀에게는 또 다른 이름이 있습니다. 하지만 나는 그냥 선생님이라는 이름이 좋고 그뿐입니다.

나는 살짝 긴장하여 웃었습니다.

"나는 그레이스에게 말 좀 전하려고 해요." 나는 매우 부드럽게 말했습니다.

선생님은 내 책상으로 서둘러 왔습니다.

"절대 *다시는* 네 의자 위로 일어서지 마, 주니 B." 그녀가 말했습니다. "네가 넘어져서 어딘가 부러질 수도 있어."

"좋았어!" 짐(Jim)이라는 이름의 못된 녀석이 소리 질렀습니다. "주니 B.가 자신의 단단한 *머리*로 *바닥*을 부술 수도 있겠네!"

나는 그 녀석을 향해 주먹을 쥐어 보였습니다.

"그리고 또 나는 **멍청이** 같은 네 머리를 전부 깨뜨릴 수도 있지!" 나는 소리치며 답했습니다.

선생님은 나를 다시 내 자리에 철퍼덕 앉혔습니다.

"그만하렴." 그녀가 짜증 내며 말했습니다. "선생님 진심이야, 주니 B. 한마디도 더 하지 마."

그 후, 나는 내 의자에 아주 얌전히 있었습니다. 그리고 나는 내 공부를 했습니다.

나는 내 철자 공부를 했습니다.

그리고 내 산수 공부도요.

그리고 내 글씨 쓰기 공부도요.

또, 나는 내 팔에 소시지 패티를 그렸습니다.

하지만 그것은 심지어 과제도 아니었습니다.

그것은 스스로 학습하기라고 불립니다.

얼마 지나지 않아, 선생님이 크게 손뼉을 쳤습니다.

"좋아요, 여러분. 이제 쉬는 시간이 거의 다 됐네요. 여러분의 활동지를 제출하고 문 앞에 줄을 서세요."

선생님이 나를 보았습니다.

"그리고 제발. . . 줄을 설 때는 신사숙녀처럼 행동합시다."

신사 숙녀는 네 이웃을 짓밟지 말라는 것을 의미합니다.

그것은 내 생각에, 십계명인 것 같아요.

나와 루실은 손을 잡았습니다.

"이제 너는 나를 소개할 거지. 그렇지, 루실? 이제 나는 그 잘생긴 남자애를 만나게 되겠네."

바로 그때, 그 그레이스가 우리 뒤로 달려왔습니다.

나는 그녀를 봐서 행복했습니다.

"그레이스! 그레이스! 이거 알아? 루실이 잘생긴 워런에게 우리를 소개할 거래! 왜냐면 너와 나는 정말로 돼지 같은 아이들이니까, 그래서 그래!"

그 그레이스는 화가 나서 나를 보았습니다.

"나는 돼지 같지 않아." 그녀가 말했습니다.

나는 재빨리 그녀의 귀에 대고 속삭였습니다. "알아, 사실 우리는 진짜로 정말 돼지 같은 사람들은 아니지, 그레이스. 우리는 그냥 우리가 정말 돼지 같다고 말하기만 하는 거야. 안 그러면 우리가 자기 남자친구를 뺏어 갈 거라고 루실이 생각하니까. 이해했지?"

그 그레이스는 이해했습니다.

"나는 진짜 불쾌하고 돼지 같은 사람이야." 그녀가 루실에게 말했습니다.

그리고 그래서 그 후, 우리 모두는 정말 행복하게 그네 세트로 깡충깡충 뛰어갔습니다.

우리는 앉았습니다. 그리고 8반 아이들이 나오기를 기다렸습니다.

우리는 아주 오랫동안 기다렸습니다.

그러다가 갑자기, 8반 아이들이 그들의 문을 열었습니다! 그리고 잘생긴 워런이 거기에서 나왔습니다!

루실은 그에게 달려가서 그의 손을 잡았습니다.

그녀는 우리를 만나게 하려고 그를 그네로 끌고 왔습니다.

"얘는 그레이스야. 그리고 얘는 주니 B. 존스고." 그녀가 잘생긴 워런에게 말했습니다.

그는 아주 귀엽고 상냥하게 손을 흔들었습니다.

나는 재빨리 내 두 손 뒤로 얼굴을 감추었습니다.

왜냐면 갑자기 내가 그 남자아이에 대해 수줍음을 느꼈기 때문입니다.

나는 내 손가락 사이로 살짝 훔쳐봤습니다.

"까꿍. 여기 있네." 내가 말했습니다.

그리고 나서 나는 웃고 또 웃었습니다. 왜냐면 나는 정말 웃긴 사람이고, 그래서 그렇죠.

나는 계속해서 그 재미있는 농담에 대해 웃었습니다.

하지만 나에게는 안타까운 일이었습니다.

왜냐면 잠시 뒤에도, 나는 멈출 수 없었기 때문입니다.

내 생각에, 나는 통제 불능이었습니다.

나는 내 옆구리를 움켜쥐고 바닥에 넘어졌습니다.

그런 다음 나는 뒹굴면서 웃고 또 뒹굴면서 웃었습니다. 잔디밭에서 이리저리 말이죠.

잘생긴 워런은 나를 보고 겁을 먹은 것 같았습니다.

그는 뒤로 물러섰습니다.

"뭐야 이 괴짜는." 그는 아주 조용히 말했습니다.

그리고 나서 그는 뒤돌았습니다. 그리고 떠나 버렸습니다.

그리고 루실과 그 그레이스도 그와 함께 걸어갔습니다.

3장 괴짜가 아니야

선생님은 호루라기를 불었습니다.

그것은 쉬는 시간이 끝났으니 들어오라는 뜻입니다.

루실과 그 그레이스는 나를 데리러 달려왔습니다.

왜냐면 내가 여전히 잔디밭 위에 있었거든요, 그래서 그렇죠.

루실은 행복해했고 생기가 가득했습니다.

"넌 워런이 정말 마음에 들지 않았니, 주니 B.? 그 애 너무 잘생기지 않았어? 걔는 가까이서 보니까 훨씬 더 잘생겼더라, 그렇게 생각하지 않아? 그 애는 또, 친절하기도 해. 걔 친절하지 않았어?"

그 그레이스도 마찬가지로, 행복해했고 생기가 가득했습니다.

"그 애는 내 하이 톱 운동화가 예쁘다고 말했어." 그녀가 내게 말했습니다.

"그 애는 내 원피스가 예쁘다고 말했어." 루실이 말했습니다.

"그 애는 내가 괴짜라고 말했어." 내가 말했습니다.

루실은 사방을 빙글빙글 돌았습니다.

"나에게는 그러지 않았지." 그녀가 말했습니다. "그 애는 나에게 괴짜라고 하지 않았어. 그건 바로 걔가 나를 좋아하기 때문이야!"

그 그레이스는 공중으로 높이 뛰었습니다.

"나도야! 또, 그 애는 나도 좋아해!" 그녀는 아주 꽥꽥거리며 말했습니다.

바로 그때, 루실은 빙글빙글 도는 것을 멈추었습니다.

그녀는 팔짱을 꼈습니다.

"아니야, 그레이스." 그녀가 말했습니다. "그 애가 또한, 너도 좋아하는 건 아니지. 그 애는 나만 좋아해. 왜냐면 내가 그 애를 먼저 봤으니까. 그리고 넌 걔를 빼앗아 가면 안 돼, 기억하지?"

그 그레이스도 마찬가지로, 자신의 팔짱을 꼈습니다.

"난 그 애를 빼앗아 가는 게 아니야, 루실. 그 애는 그냥 자기도 모르게 스스로 나를 좋아하는 거지. 그리고 그렇게 된 것에 대해서는 내가 할 수 있는 일이 없어." 그녀가 말했습니다.

나는 루실의 원피스를 잡아당겼습니다.

"어째서 그 애는 나를 괴짜라고 했을까, 어떻게 생각해? 왜 그 애는 그런 바보 같은 말을 해야 했던 걸까?"

루실은 나를 거들떠보지도 않았습니다. 그녀는 계속해서 그 그레이스에게 화를 내고 있었습니다.

"그럼 그렇지!" 그녀가 투덜거렸습니다. "난 이렇게 될 줄 알았어, 그레이스!

너는 내 남자친구를 빼앗으려 하고 있잖아! 주니 B.는 네가 그러지 않을 거라고 했단 말이야! 그런데 넌 그러고 있어!"

그녀는 나를 내려다봤습니다.

"얘한테 말해, 주니 B.! 그레이스에게 자기가 내 남자친구를 빼앗을 수 없다고 말해!"

나는 의아하다는 듯이 그녀를 보았습니다.

"나는 괴짜가 아니야. 아닌가? 내가 괴짜야?" 내가 말했습니다. "난 괴짜가 아닌데."

바로 그때, 그 그레이스는 루실의 코 쪽으로 바짝 몸을 기울였습니다.

"나는 내가 원하는 누구든 좋아할 수 있어, 루실!" 그녀는 루실의 얼굴에 대고 소리쳤습니다.

"아니, 넌 그럴 수 없어, 그레이스!"

"아니, 나도 *마찬가지로*, 그럴 수 있어, 루실!"

나는 그 둘의 발목을 톡톡 쳤습니다.

"몇 명이나 나를 괴짜라고 생각하는 거니? 손 들어 봐." 내가 말했습니다.

바로 그때, 선생님은 다시 그녀의 호루라기를 불었습니다.

그리고 그래서 나는 잔디밭에서 일어났습니다. 그리고 나는 혼자서 9반으로 걸어갔습니다.

왜냐면 나는 괴짜인 것에 대한 생각

을 멈출 수 없었고, 그래서 그렇죠.

나는 남은 하루 내내 그것에 대해 생각했습니다.

나는 말도 하지 않았습니다.

발표 시간에도요.

간식 시간에도요.

심지어 내가 집으로 가려고 버스에 탔을 때도요.

그 그레이스는 내 옆에 앉았습니다. 그녀는 다시 행복해했고 생기가 가득했습니다.

"나는 그 애가 루실보다 나를 더 좋아한다는 걸 알아." 그녀가 말했습니다. "난 걔가 그럴 거라고 확신해. 그리고 그 애는 내가 얼마나 빨리 달릴 수 있는지 아직 보지도 못했잖아."

그녀는 자기 손가락으로 나를 찔렀습니다.

"네 생각에는 그 애가 누구를 더 좋아하는 거 같아? 나야 아니면 루실이야? 그리고 사실대로 말해 봐." 그녀가 말했습니다.

나는 여전히 말하지 않았습니다.

그 그레이스는 나를 흔들었습니다.

"어째서 너는 말하지 않는 거야, 주니 B.?" 그녀가 물었습니다. "어째서 넌 내 말에 대답하지 않는 거야? 너 아파? 너 목이 아프니?"

바로 그때, 그녀의 눈이 아주 크게 휘둥그레졌습니다. 그리고 그녀의 입이 떡 벌어졌습니다.

"오오오오. . . 난 왜 네가 말하지 않는 건지 알겠어. 그건 바로 네가 화났기 때문이야, 그렇지? 너는 네가 괴짜라는 사실에 화가 난 거야."

나는 그녀를 향해 아주 재빨리 몸을 돌렸습니다.

"나는 괴짜가 아니야, 그레이스! 난 그냥 평범하고 정상인 여자아이야. 그리고 나는 왜 그 남자애가 날 그렇게 불러야 했던 건지도 전혀 모르겠다고!"

"나는 알겠던데." 그 그레이스가 말했습니다. "나는 왜 그 애가 너를 그렇게 불렀는지 알아. 그건 네가 웃음을 멈출 수 없었기 때문이야. 그리고 너는 잔디밭에 넘어졌고. 그리고 너는 그 아래에서 이리저리 굴러다녔잖아."

나는 그녀를 빤히 쳐다봤습니다.

"응? 그래서?" 내가 말했습니다.

"그러니까 괴짜들이 그렇게 행동한다는 거지." 그 그레이스가 말했습니다. "그리고 나는 잘 알 수밖에 없어. 왜냐면 바로 우리 개인적인 가족 중에 괴짜가 있거든."

나는 내 눈썹을 치켜올렸습니다.

"그래?" 내가 말했습니다.

"그래." 그녀가 말했습니다. "내 두 살짜리 남동생 제피(Jeffie)가 괴짜야. 우리가 쇼핑몰에 갈 때마다, 우리는 개한테 목줄을 매야 해. 안 그랬다간 개가

사람들에게 덤벼들 테니까. 그리고 그러면 개는 옷 사이에 숨고 경비원이 오게 되거든."

그녀는 나를 아주 의심스럽게 쳐다봤습니다..

"너도 언젠가 그런 적 있니, 주니 B. 존스? 흐음? 너도 사람들에게 달려든 적 있어? 그리고 옷 사이에 숨어서 경비원이 와야 했고?"

나는 재빠르게 그녀에게서 고개를 돌렸습니다.

왜냐면 그것은 나의 개인적인 일이기 때문입니다.

"제피는 또, 설탕이 들어간 시리얼도 더 이상 먹어서는 안 돼." 그 그레이스가 말했습니다. "우리 엄마는 설탕이 개를 정말 흥분시킨다고 생각하거든."

그녀는 몹시 궁금하다는 듯이 한쪽 눈썹을 치켜올렸습니다.

"넌 아침으로 설탕이 든 시리얼을 먹니, 주니 B.? 흐음? 너도 *그러는 거야?*" 그녀가 물었습니다.

나는 또 한 번 눈길을 돌렸습니다.

왜냐면 맞춰 볼래요?

나의 개인적인 일이 더 나왔거든요. 바로 그거예요.

4장 식이 섬유

다음 날 아침이었습니다.

나는 티클에게 설탕이 든 내 시리얼을 주었습니다.

나는 녀석에게 나의 스위티 퍼프(Sweetie Puffs)를 주었습니다. 그리고 나의 크래클 베리(Crackle Berries)도요. 그리고 나의 해피 스매키 플레이크(Happy Smacky Flakes)도요.

티클은 그런 것들을 먹는 걸 정말 많이 좋아했습니다.

그런 다음 녀석은 거실 안을 뛰어다녔습니다. 그리고 녀석은 양탄자 위에 토했습니다.

엄마는 아주 크게 소리 질렀습니다.

그게 바로 내가 싱크대 아래로 숨었던 이유입니다. 하지만 엄마와 아빠는 그곳에서 나를 찾았습니다.

그들은 그렇게 능숙하게 자신들을 자제하지 못했습니다.

"왜, 주니 B.? 도대체 왜 그런 짓을 하려 한 거야!" 아빠가 아주 시끄럽게 소리 질렀습니다.

"우리가 매 순간 너를 지켜봐야 하는 거니?" 엄마가 아주 시끄럽게 소리 질렀습니다.

바로 그때, 나의 헬렌 밀러(Helen Miller) 할머니가 현관문으로 걸어 들어왔습니다.

"밀러 할머니(Grandma Miller)! 밀러 할머니! 사랑해요! 사랑해요!" 내가 외쳤습니다.

그러고 나서 나는 아주 재빠르게 그녀를 향해 달려갔습니다. 그리고 나는 엄마와 아빠가 일하러 나갈 때까지 그녀의 코트 속에 숨었습니다.

그 후, 나의 할머니는 내게 새로 먹을 시리얼을 고르게 했습니다.

나는 어른들이 먹는 종류로 골랐습니다.

그것은 그 안에 식이 섬유가 든 종류였습니다.

"이런 종류가 나에게 좋은 거예요. 맞죠, 할머니? 이런 종류는 날 흥분시키지도 않을 거예요."

그런 다음 나는 그 맛있는 것을 내 입 안에 넣었습니다.

그리고 나는 씹고 또 씹었습니다. 하지만 그 시리얼은 사실 그렇게 잘 부스러지지는 않았습니다.

나는 그것을 아침 내내 씹었습니다.

나는 그 그레이스가 내 스쿨버스에 탔을 때도 여전히 씹고 있었습니다.

그녀는 아주 신이 나서 내게 달려왔습니다.

"이것 봐, 주니 B.! 우리 엄마가 나에게 뭘 사 주었는지 봐!" 그녀가 말했습니다.

그녀는 그녀의 발을 들어 올렸습니

다.

"새 운동화야!" 그녀가 말했습니다. "이것들 보여? 옆면에 있는 번개 모양 줄무늬 좀 봐! 이건 내가 번개처럼 빠르게 달릴 수 있다는 의미지! 그리고 그래서 이제 워런은 분명 나를 가장 좋아하게 될 거야!"

나는 내 입을 손가락으로 가리켰습니다.

"좋아, 하지만 나는 사실 이 문제를 지금 당장 이야기할 수 없어, 그레이스. 왜냐하면 나는 여기에서 식이 섬유를 씹고 있거든." 내가 말했습니다.

나는 그녀에게 보여 주기 위해 입을 벌렸습니다.

"그것들이 이 안에 있는 게 보이지? 내 생각에, 그것들이 내 이에 끼인 것 같아."

그 후, 나는 내 손톱으로 사방을 쑤셨습니다. 그리고 나는 식이 섬유를 빨아 먹었습니다.

나는 입을 쩝쩝댔습니다.

"좋은 소식이야. 내 생각엔 내가 다 먹은 것 같아." 내가 말했습니다.

그 그레이스는 다시 한번 내게 자기 신발을 보여 주려 했습니다.

"좋아, 그런데 유감이야, 그레이스. 그렇지만 난 여전히 아직 말할 수 없는 걸. 왜냐하면 내가 정말 중요한 걸 해야 하기 때문이야."

그리고 나서 나는 내 자리에서 몸을 뒤로 기대었습니다.

그리고 나는 내 두 눈을 감았습니다.

그리고 나는 오랫동안 움직이지 않았습니다.

갑자기, 나는 정말 기뻐서 손뼉을 쳤습니다.

"너 나 봤어, 그레이스? 내가 방금 얼마나 차분하게 있었는지 봤니? 그건 오늘 내 몸 안에 설탕이 없기 때문이야! 그리고 나는 아주 훌륭하게 가만히 앉아 있을 수 있지!"

나는 그녀를 아주 세게 껴안았습니다.

"효과가 있었어, 그레이스! 식이 섬유 시리얼이 효과가 있었다고! 이제 나는 더 이상 괴짜가 아니야! 그리고 그래서 잘생긴 워런은 꼭 그가 널 좋아하는 것처럼 나도 좋아할 거야!"

그 그레이스는 행복해 보이지 않았습니다.

그녀는 아래로 몸을 숙여 그녀의 새 신발에서 먼지를 털었습니다.

나는 그녀를 따라 아래로 몸을 숙였습니다.

"어째서 너는 행복해하지 않는 거야, 그레이스? 왜 너는 그 애가 마찬가지로, 나도 좋아할 거라는 이야기에 행복해하지 않는 거야?" 내가 물었습니다.

그녀는 씩씩댔습니다.

"너 신발에 입김을 내뿜고 있어." 그녀가 말했습니다. "신발에 대고 숨 쉬지 마."

바로 그때, 버스가 학교에서 멈췄습니다.

나는 창밖을 보고 몹시 흥분해서 손뼉을 쳤습니다.

"그레이스! 그레이스! 나 잘생긴 워런이 보여! 그 애는 지금 식수대에 있어! 그리고 루실은 아직 거기에 있지 않아!"

갑자기 그 그레이스의 얼굴에는 생기가 넘쳤습니다.

그녀는 재빠른 총알처럼 급히 버스에서 내렸습니다. 그리고 그녀는 잘생긴 워런에게 아주 잽싸게 뛰어갔습니다.

나는 그녀가 온 운동장에 내지르는 목소리를 들을 수 있었습니다.

"이것 봐, 워런! 내 새 신발 좀 봐!" 그녀가 소리쳤습니다. "그것들은 옆에 번개가 있다고! 보이지?"

그녀는 그 잘생긴 남자아이 주변으로 원을 그리며 달리고 있었습니다.

"달리기 시합할래?" 그녀가 그에게 물었습니다. "내가 얼마나 빠른지 볼래? 틀림없이 넌 날 이길 수 없어, 워런! 틀림없이 넌 달리기 시합에서 날 이길 수 없다고!"

그리고 그래서 바로 그때, 잘생긴 워런과 그 그레이스는 온 운동장을 빠르게 달렸습니다.

그리고 그는 그녀를 이기지도 못했습니다.

그는 아주 녹초가 되어 돌아왔습니다.

"와." 그가 말했습니다. "너는 내가 지금까지 본 사람 중 가장 빠른 달리기 선수야. 어쩌면 나중에 네가 올림픽(Olympics)에 나갈지도 모르겠다."

"난 그럴 거야, 워런!" 그 그레이스가 말했습니다. "나는 언젠가 올림픽에 나갈 거야! 나랑 다시 달리기 시합할래? 응? 해 볼래?"

바로 그때, 루실이 갑자기 튀어나왔습니다.

그녀는 내가 지금까지 본 것 중 가장 예쁜 원피스를 입고 있었습니다.

그녀는 사방을 빙빙 돌았습니다.

"오오오오, 루실. 너 그거 입으니까 공주 전하처럼 보인다." 내가 말했습니다.

"나도 알아." 그녀가 말했습니다. "이건 공주님이 입는 종류의 원피스야. 이건 비싼 빨간색 벨벳(velvet)으로 만들어졌어."

그녀는 잘생긴 워런 앞에서 빙글빙글 돌았습니다.

"이 원피스는 150달러도 넘어. . . 세금은 *빼고*." 그녀가 말했습니다.

갑자기, 잘생긴 워런의 눈이 휘둥그레졌습니다.

"우와! 넌 이 학교 전체에서 제일 부자인 여자애겠다!" 그가 말했습니다.

루실은 그녀의 머리를 부풀렸습니다.

"맞아." 그녀가 말했습니다. "나는 진짜로 이 학교 전체에서 가장 부자인 아이야, 워런. 이 신발은 얼마인지 한번 맞혀 볼래? 그냥 맞혀 봐, 어때?"

바로 그때 나는 그 남자아이의 얼굴 바로 앞으로 뛰어들었습니다.

"안녕. 오늘 기분 어때?" 나는 아주 상냥하게 말했습니다. "난 기분이 좋아. 난 기분이 좋고 차분하지."

그는 나에게서 물러섰습니다.

"좋아, 그런데 네가 겁먹을 필요는 없어." 내가 말했습니다. "왜냐면 나는 아침으로 식이 섬유을 먹었거든. 그리고 아마도, 나는 너무 차분해져서 잠들 수도 있을 것 같아. 나를 한번 볼래? 응, 워런? 내가 잠드는 거 볼래?"

나는 잔디밭에 털썩하고 누웠습니다.

"봐, 워런. 내가 여기 아래에 있는 게 보여? 나는 심지어 웃거나 뒹굴고 있지도 않아. 나는 그냥 차분하게 있을 뿐이야. 그리고 그게 다야."

나는 땅바닥 위에 내 머리를 내려놓았습니다.

"내가 잠드는 걸 봐, 워런. 나를 봐. 나 좀 보라고."

나는 내 두 눈을 감았다가 다시 떴습니다.

"너 방금 봤어, 워런? 응? 너 내가 잠드는 거 봤어? 맞지? 내가 너에게 나 차분하다고 말했잖아. 안 그래? 응? 내가 너한테 말하지 않았어?"

잘생긴 워런이 나를 보고 또 보았습니다.

그리고 나서 그는 그의 손가락을 머리 옆에서 빙빙 돌렸습니다.

그리고 그는 그녀로 걸어가 버렸습니다.

그리고 루실과 그 그레이스는 그 애와 함께 걸어갔습니다.

5장 공주님 옷 만세!

그날 밤 저녁 식사 시간에, 훌륭한 생각이 내 머릿속에 떠올랐습니다.

그 생각은 내가 마카로니(macaroni)를 먹던 중에 떠올랐습니다.

"저기요! 나 방금 그게 생각났어요!" 내가 외쳤습니다. "나 방금 그 잘생긴 남자애가 나를 좋아하게 할 방법을 생각해 냈어요!"

나는 더 많은 마카로니를 입에 쑤셔 넣었습니다.

"빨리요, 여러분! 먹어요! 먹어! 우

리는 쇼핑몰이 문을 닫기 전에 가야 해요!"

바로 그때, 마카로니 두 개가 내 입 밖으로 떨어져 나왔습니다. 그리고 바닥으로 말이죠. 그리고 티클이라는 이름의 내 강아지가 그것들을 먹었습니다.

아빠는 얼굴을 찌푸렸습니다.

"얘, 얘, 얘! 천천히 해! 뭐가 그렇게 급해?" 그가 말했습니다.

"우린 쇼핑몰로 가야 해요! 바로 그게 급한 일이에요! 우리는 나에게 공주님 원피스를 사 주어야 해요! 그리고 또 나는 번개가 그려진 신발도 필요하고요!"

엄마와 아빠는 나를 이상한 표정으로 바라보았습니다.

그래서 내가 잘생긴 워런에 대해 전부 설명해야 했던 것입니다. 그리고 그가 루실의 공주님 원피스를 얼마나 좋아했는지에 대해서도요. 그리고 그가 그레이스의 잽싼 신발을 얼마나 좋아했는지도요.

"그리고 그래서 이제 나도 공주님 원피스를 살 거예요! 그리고 또 나는 번개가 그려진 신발도 살 거예요! 그리고 그러면 워런은 또, 나도 좋아하겠죠!"

나는 내 손으로 내 입을 닦았습니다. 그런 다음 나는 빠르게 내 의자에서 뛰어내렸습니다.

"실례할게요! 식탁에서 먼저 일어날게요! 왜냐하면 나는 정말 배부르거든요!"

나는 복도를 따라 달렸습니다. 그리고 아기방으로 쌩 하고 뛰어 들어갔습니다.

아기방은 올리(Ollie)라는 이름의 내 남동생이 사는 곳입니다.

"엄마 아빠는 설거지해요!" 나는 엄마와 아빠에게 소리쳤습니다. "나는 올리의 스웨터를 그 애 머리에 씌울게요! 왜냐하면 그렇게 하는 게 우리의 시간을 절약해 줄 테니까요, 내 생각에는요!"

나는 재빨리 올리의 아기 침대 안으로 올라갔습니다.

그러고 나서 나는 올리의 스웨터를 그에게 입히려 했습니다. 하지만 그의 거대한 머리는 구멍에 맞지 않았습니다.

그는 낮잠에서 깼습니다.

그런 다음 그는 아주 시끄럽게 울기 시작했습니다.

나는 복도에서 시끄럽게 발이 달려오는 소리를 들었습니다.

"주니 B. 존스! 너 도대체 뭐 하고 있는 거니?" 화난 목소리가 고함쳤습니다.

그것은 엄마의 목소리였습니다.

그녀는 방 안으로 뛰어 들어왔습니다. 그리고 아기 올리를 들어 올렸습니다.

그녀는 그의 거대한 머리를 쓰다듬었습니다.

"그는 정말 멜론처럼 큰 머리를 가지고 있네요." 나는 아주 조용히 말했습니다.

아기 올리는 계속해서 울었습니다.

"내가 목줄을 가져올까요?" 나는 엄마에게 물었습니다. "우리 올리에게 목줄을 매는 거예요, 어때요? 왜냐면 내 생각에, 얘는 몹시 흥분한 것 같거든요. 그리고 그러니 어떻게 우리가 쇼핑몰에서 얘를 통제할 수 있겠어요?"

엄마는 그녀의 머리 저 뒤쪽으로 자신의 두 눈을 굴렸습니다.

"우린 쇼핑몰에 안 갈 *거야*, 주니 B." 그녀가 말했습니다. "우리는 아무 데도 안 갈 거야."

나는 내 발을 쿵쿵 굴렀습니다.

"갈 거예요!" 내가 말했습니다. "우리는 가야 해요! 우리는 내 공주님 원피스를 사러 쇼핑몰에 *가야* 한다고요! 그리고 번개가 그려진 내 신발도요. 안 그러면 그 남자애가 날 좋아하지 않을 거란 말이에요, 정말이에요!"

엄마는 자신의 두 눈을 감았습니다. 그녀는 깊은 심호흡을 몇 번 했습니다.

그녀의 목소리가 더 부드러워졌습니다.

"알겠어. 엄마는 네가 엄마 말을 들

어 줬으면 한단다. 그리고 엄마는 네가 귀담아들어 줬으면 해." 그녀가 말했습니다. "너는 새 원피스를 입거나 번개가 그려진 신발을 신는 것으로 친구를 사귀는 게 아니란다. 너는 함께 있으면 즐거운 사람이 되어서 새로운 친구를 사귀는 거야. 그리고 사람들에게 친절하게 대하는 것으로 말이지. 그리고 그들의 기분에 신경 쓰는 것으로 말이야."

그녀는 나를 아기 침대 밖으로 들어 올렸습니다.

"그리고 또, *정직함*도 중요하단다, 주니 B." 그녀가 말했습니다. "너는 사람들에게 반드시 *정직해야* 해. 그리고 그건 네가 너 자신이 아닌 다른 누군가인 척할 수 없다는 뜻이야."

그녀는 내 머리를 쓰다듬었습니다.

"너는 루실이 *아니잖아*, 주니 B. 그리고 마찬가지로, 너는 그레이스도 아니야. 너는 그냥 *너야*. 너는 그냥 주니 B. 존스인 거야. 그리고 엄마 말을 믿으렴, 그건 누구에게나 정말 중요한 일이야."

나는 코를 훌쩍였습니다. 또 나는 코를 쿵쿵거리고 삼켰습니다.

"좋아요, 하지만 나는 내가 주니 B. 존스라는 걸 *알아요*." 내가 말했습니다. "나는 그냥 공주님 원피스를 입은 주니 B. 존스가 되고 싶은 거예요."

나는 엄마의 어깨에 내 머리를 기대었습니다.

"엄마가 어렸을 때 엄마는 공주님 원피스를 입어 보고 싶었던 적 없었어요?" 내가 물었습니다. "네, 엄마? 엄마는 그런 적 없었어요?"

엄마는 대답하지 않았습니다. 그녀는 아마 내 질문에 대해 곰곰이 생각하고 있었을 거예요.

바로 그때, 나는 그녀의 어깨 너머를 보았습니다.

나는 아기 올리의 선반 위에 있는 새 장난감을 보았습니다.

"엄마! 저건 뭐예요, 엄마? 저기 선반 위에 있는 건 뭐죠? 내가 보고 있는 게 새 곰 인형인가요?"

나는 달려가서 그 녀석을 끌어내렸습니다.

"봐요, 엄마! 이 곰 인형이 달고 있는 것 좀 봐요! 그건 비싼, 빨간색 벨벳으로 만들어진 리본이에요! 그리고 저건 정확히(zactly) 내가 찾던 종류의 옷감이에요!"

나는 그 곰 인형에게서 리본을 뗐습니다. 그리고 나는 그 리본을 내 머리 옆에 댔습니다.

"나 어때 보여요? 네, 엄마? 내가 예쁜 공주님처럼 보이나요? 나 멋져 보여요? 네? 그래요?"

바로 그때, 나는 마음속으로 행복해졌고 생기가 가득해졌습니다.

나는 빠르게 엄마에게 뽀뽀하고 방을 잽싸게 빠져나갔습니다.

왜냐면 어쩌면 바로 우리 집 안에 공주님 옷이 더 있을지도 모르니까요!

6장 말문이 막히는 일

다음 날, 그 그레이스는 버스에서 나를 보았습니다.

그녀의 입이 떡 하고 벌어졌습니다.

나는 아주 우아하게 미소 지었습니다.

"나는 네가 왜 나를 그렇게 보고 있는지 알아, 그레이스." 내가 말했습니다. "엄마가 말했는데 사람들이 나를 보면, 말문이 막힐 거래."

나는 내 머리를 부풀렸습니다.

"말문이 막히는 건 네 입이 말할 수 없다는 거야." 내가 설명했습니다.

그 그레이스가 내 목을 가리켰습니다.

"그건 뭐야? 네가 하고 있는 게 개 목걸이니?" 그녀가 말했습니다.

나는 그녀를 보고 웃고 또 웃었습니다.

"너 정말 바보구나, 그레이스!" 내가 말했습니다. "너 정말 모르겠니? 이건 보석이 달린 멋진 목걸이잖아! 이건 공주님이 하는 그런 종류의 장신구야! 하지만 나는 우리 집에 이런 멋진 물건이 있는지도 몰랐지! 나는 이걸 엄마가 강아지 사료를 두는 곳에서 발견했어. 하지만 사실 나는 왜 이게 그곳에 놓여 있었는지 잘 모르겠어."

나는 내 두 팔을 내밀었습니다.

"그리고 너 이거 알아챘니, 그레이스? 너 내 길고 하얀 공주님 장갑을 눈치챘어? 이건 신데렐라(Cinderella)가 끼는 종류의 장갑이야. 그리고 신데렐라는 진짜, 실제 공주님이야. 그리고 또 신데렐라는 바닥을 닦지."

나는 내 머리를 가리켰습니다.

"그리고 내가 쓰고 있는 이 금색 왕관은 어때? 이건 진짜 실제 데어리퀸(Dairy Queen)에서 가져온 거야! 그리고, 또 나는 내 운동화에 빨간색 벨벳 리본을 달았어! 그리고 엄마는 심지어 운동화 옆면에 번개 모양도 그려 주었어. 딱 네 것처럼 말이야!"

나는 사방을 빙글빙글 돌았습니다.

"이제 잘생긴 워런이 날 보기만 하면 돼! 그렇지, 그레이스? 이제 그 남자애는 나를 좋아하게 될 거거든! 왜냐면 누가 안 그러겠어?"

그레이스는 그녀의 자리에 털썩 앉았습니다.

그녀는 학교로 가는 길 내내 말하지 않았습니다.

그리고 또 이거 아세요? 버스가 학교에 도착했을 때, 그녀는 또 나를 기다려 주지도 않았습니다.

그녀는 나를 빼고 잘생긴 워런에게로 곧장 달려갔습니다.

나는 그녀와 시합하려 했습니다. 하지만 보석이 달린 내 목걸이가 나의 목을 긁었습니다. 그리고 또 내 금색 왕관이 내 머리에서 떨어졌습니다.

잘생긴 워런은 땅바닥에 앉아 있었습니다.

그의 얼굴은 그의 무릎에 감추어져 있었습니다.

나는 루실과 그 그레이스 앞으로 밀치며 나갔습니다.

그런 다음 나는 그의 머리를 톡톡 쳤습니다.

"안녕. 오늘 기분 어때? 나는 공주님 옷을 입고 있어." 내가 그에게 말했습니다.

잘생긴 워런은 올려다보지 않았습니다.

나는 다시 한번 그의 머리를 톡톡 쳤습니다.

"좋아, 그런데 난 사실 네가 나를 좀 봐야 한다고 생각하거든. 왜냐면 밀러 할머니가 말하길 내가 꽤나 구경거리래." 내가 말했습니다.

루실은 자신의 두 눈을 굴렸습니다.

"개한테 말을 거는 건 너에게 전혀 좋을 게 없을 거야, 주니 B." 그녀가 말했습니다. "그는 지금 누구하고도 말하지 않고 있어."

"심지어 나에게도 말이야." 그 그레이스가 말했습니다.

나는 그 남자아이 옆에 쪼그리고 앉았습니다. 그리고 정말 아주 빤히 쳐다보았습니다.

"어째서 너는 말을 안 하는 거야? 응, 워런? 고양이가 네 혀를 물어 갔니?"

나는 정말 참을성 있게 기다렸습니다.

그러고 나서 나는 그의 귀 쪽으로 더 가까이 몸을 기울였습니다.

"내가 말했잖아, 고양이가 네 혀를 물어 간 거니, 워런?"

갑자기, 잘생긴 워런이 자신의 고개를 들었습니다.

"저리 가!" 그가 고함쳤습니다. "너희 전부! 저리 가서 나를 좀 내버려 둬!"

나는 아주 오랫동안 계속해서 쪼그리고 있었습니다.

그런 다음 나는 매우 조용히 일어섰습니다. 그리고 나는 그 그레이스와 루실을 보았습니다.

"좋은 소식이야." 내가 말했습니다. "얘가 말했어."

그 후, 우리 모두는 계속해서 거기서 있었고 또 거기 서 있었습니다.

왜냐면 우리는 사실 이런 상황에 어떻게 대처하면 좋을지 몰랐기 때문이고, 그래서 그렇습니다.

마침내, 루실은 그에게 씩씩댔습니다.

"넌 친절하게 굴지 않는구나, 워런. 넌 원래 친절했었지. 하지만 지금 넌 그렇지 않아. 그리고 그래서 난 심지어 오늘 네 친구가 되고 싶지도 않아."

"나도, 마찬가지야." 그 그레이스가 말했습니다. "나도 마찬가지로, 오늘 네 친구가 되고 싶지 않아!"

그 후 그 두 녀석은 손을 잡았습니다. 그리고 그들은 매우 화가 나서 그곳에서 쿵쿵거리며 떠났습니다.

잘생긴 워런은 그들이 갔는지 보기 위해 한쪽 눈을 떴습니다.

나는 빠르게 몸을 숙여서 그 눈을 들여다보았습니다.

"안녕. 오늘 기분 어때?" 내가 말했습니다. "나는 공주님 옷을 입고 있어."

잘생긴 워런이 끙 하는 소리를 냈습니다.

그러고 나서 그는 눈을 감았습니다. 그리고 그는 또 한 번 자신의 얼굴을 숨겼습니다.

7장 똑똑

나는 잘생긴 워런 옆에 앉았습니다.

"그거 알아? 나는 너를 전혀 귀찮게 하지 않을 거야." 내가 말했습니다. "나는 그냥 여기 앉아만 있을 거야. 그리고 내 개인적인 일만 신경 쓸게. 그리고 그게 다야."

나는 조금 생각했습니다.

"그리고 여기 또 하나 좋은 소식이 있어. 너는 네가 원하지 않는다면 내 공주님 옷을 보지 않아도 돼. 왜냐면 옷은 내가 친구를 사귀는 방법이 아니니까." 내가 말했습니다.

잘생긴 워런은 움직이지 않았습니다.

나는 그의 머리를 바라보았습니다.

"그거 알아? 네 머리카락 속에 뭔가 있어." 내가 그에게 말했습니다.

나는 그것을 더 자세히 쳐다보았습니다.

"내 생각에 그건 작은 잎사귀 같아. 그게 아니라면 휴지 조각일지도 모르지." 내가 말했습니다.

그는 여전히 움직이지 않았습니다.

"내가 너 대신 그걸 털어 줄까?" 내가 물었습니다. "왜냐면 그건 전혀 어려운 일이 아니거든. 그리고 나는 기꺼이 그렇게 할 수 있어."

나는 아주 참을성 있게 그가 대답하기를 기다렸습니다.

그러고 나서 나는 그를 조금 더 톡톡 쳤습니다.

"좋아, 그런데 난 정말 네가 뭐라도 해야 한다고 생각해." 내가 말했습니다. "왜냐면 만약 누군가 그 자그마한 휴지에 코를 풀었던 거라면? 그리고 그다음에 그 휴지가 바람에 날아갔던 거지. 그리고 네 머리에 붙어 버린 거야. 너 이런 거 생각해 본 적 있어? 응? 왜냐면 그건 유쾌하지는 않을 것 같거든."

그는 대답하지 않았습니다.

"내가 그의 머리카락에서 휴지를 뗐으면 하는 사람, 손 들어 보세요." 내가 말했습니다.

갑자기, 잘생긴 워런이 그의 화난 얼굴을 드러냈습니다.

"나는 네가 말하지 않을 거라고 생각했는데!" 그가 소리쳤습니다. "난 네가 네 개인적인 일만 신경 쓸 거라고 생각했어!"

나는 정말 귀엽게 미소 지었습니다.

"응, 그런데 난 내 개인적인 일만 신경 쓰는 중이야, 워런." 내가 말했습니다. "나는 그냥 너에게 작은 휴지에 대해 말해 줄 필요가 있었던 것뿐이야. 그리고 그래서 나 이제 말 다 했어. 끝이야. 이야기 끝."

잘생긴 워런은 저 하늘 위로 멀리 그의 눈을 굴렸습니다. 그는 또 한 번 그의 두 팔로 가렸습니다.

나는 조금 더 기다렸습니다.

"알겠어, 한 가지 문제가 있어." 내가 말했습니다. "작은 휴지가 여전히 거기에 있는걸. 그리고 그러니까 넌 내가 이 휴지를 어떻게 처리해 줬으면 해?"

잘생긴 워런은 자기 두 귀를 자신의 두 손으로 막았습니다.

"그만 좀 해!" 그가 소리쳤습니다. "나한테 그만 말해! 그나저나 넌 왜 여기에 앉아 있는 거야? 그냥 네 멍청한 친구들이랑 같이 가서 나를 좀 내버려 두지 그래?"

"왜냐면 나는 친절하게 굴고 있거든, 그래서 그래." 내가 말했습니다. "그리고 또 나는 네 기분을 이해하려는 거야. 왜냐하면 그렇게 하는 것이 내가 친구를 사귀는 방법이라고 엄마가 말했거든."

잘생긴 워런은 불만 가득한 표정을 지었습니다.

"나는 네 친구가 *아니야*." 그가 말했습니다. "나는 이 학교에 친구가 아무도 없어. 내 친구들은 전부 내가 다녔던 다른 학교에 있었어. 하지만 그때 우리 아빠가 나를 여기로 전학 오게 했어. 그리고 이제 아무것도 전과 같지 않아. 나는 이곳이 너무 싫어! 난 여기가 싫어! 난 여기가 싫다고!"

그런 다음 그는 다시 한번 그의 얼굴을 자신의 무릎에 묻었습니다. 그리고 그는 울기 시작했습니다.

그는 조용히 하려고 했습니다.

하지만 나는 여전히 그가 그 안에서 훌쩍거리는 소리를 들을 수 있었습니다.

그것은 내 마음을 슬프게 했습니다.

나는 그를 아주 부드럽게 토닥였습니다.

"안됐다, 워런. 네 기분이 안 좋다니 유감이야. 정말 안타까워. 유감이야." 내가 매우 부드럽게 말했습니다.

바로 그때 좋은 생각 하나가 내 머릿속에 떠올랐습니다.

"있지. 나 알겠어. 어쩌면 내가 너에게 반창고를 가져다줄 수도 있어. 어때, 워런? 왜냐면 가끔 반창고는 상황을 더 나아지게 하거든. . ."

"아니면 여기 좋은 생각이 하나 더 있어. 어쩌면 내가 너를 간지럽힐 수도 있어. 왜냐면 간지럽히는 건 너를 웃게 할 테니까, 맞지? 그리고 그래서 내가 기꺼이 한번 해 볼게."

나는 그를 흔들었습니다.

"내 금색 왕관 써 볼래, 워런? 응? 써 볼래? 왜냐면 금색 왕관은 네 기분을 아주 좋게 하거든."

나는 그에게 주려고 왕관을 벗었습니다.

그는 그것을 받지 않았습니다.

나는 땅바닥에 내 금색 왕관을 내려놓았습니다.

그러고 나서 나는 내 공주님 목걸이와 내 신데렐라 장갑을 벗었습니다. 그리고 또, 나는 그것들도 땅바닥에 놓았습니다.

그 후, 나는 아주 가만히 앉아 있었습니다. 그리고 나는 워런이 슬퍼하는 소리를 들었습니다.

마침내 나는 한숨을 쉬었습니다. 그리고 나는 정말 최후의 방법을 시도했습니다.

"똑똑." 내가 말했습니다.

잘생긴 워런은 대답하지 않았습니다.

"똑똑." 나는 조금 더 크게 말했습니다. 그리고 나서 나는 계속해서 똑똑이라고 말했는데, 그 남자아이가 그 소리에 싫증이 날 때까지 말이죠.

"으, 알았어! 누구세요?" 그가 툴툴대며 말했습니다.

"헤취(hatch)예요." 내가 말했습니다.

"헤취?" 잘생긴 워런이 말했습니다.

"하하! 내가 널 재채기하게 했어! 이해돼, 워런? 이해돼? 네가 *헤취*라고 했잖아! 이해되지?"

"똑똑." 나는 또 한 번 말했습니다.

잘생긴 워런이 한쪽 눈으로 나를 살짝 보았습니다.

"누구세요?" 그가 말했습니다.

"에쉬(ash)예요." 내가 말했습니다.

"에쉬?" 잘생긴 워런이 말했습니다.

"하! 내가 또 해냈어, 워런! 내가 너를 또 한 번 재채기하게 했지! 네가 *에쉬*라고 말했잖아! 그리고 그래서 방금 것도 또 하나의 괜찮은 농담이었

어, 그렇지?"

잘생긴 워런이 그의 고개를 들었습니다. 그의 얼굴은 전처럼 화나 보이지 않았습니다.

"똑똑." 내가 말했습니다.

"누구세요?" 잘생긴 워런이 말했습니다.

"쿡(kook)이에요."

"쿡?" 그가 말했습니다.

나는 그 남자아이를 향해 주먹을 쥐어 보였습니다.

"야! 넌 누구를 바보(cuckoo)라고 비웃는 거야, 응?" 내가 말했습니다.

바로 그때, 잘생긴 워런이 살짝 미소 지었습니다.

그는 잠깐 기다렸습니다. 그런 다음 그는 조금 더 미소 지었습니다.

"똑똑." 그가 말했습니다.

"누구세요?"

"아이시(icy)예요." 잘생긴 워런이 말했습니다.

"아이시?"

"저는 런던이 보여요, 저는 프랑스가 보이고요, 저는 루실의 속바지가 보인다고요." 그가 말했습니다.

나는 박수 치고 또 쳤습니다.

"나도, 워런! 나도 마찬가지로, 루실의 속바지를 봤어! 왜냐면 그 이상한 괴짜는 항상 그런 펄럭거리는 원피스를 입고 빙글빙글 도는데, 그래서 그렇

지!"

갑자기, 나의 얼굴 전체가 밝아졌습니다.

"똑똑!"

"누구세요?" 잘생긴 워런이 말했습니다.

"아이리시(Irish)예요."

"아이리시?"

"저는 오스카 마이어의 소시지였으면 좋겠어요!" 나는 아주 시끄럽게 노래를 불렀습니다.

그리고 나서 나와 잘생긴 워런은 아주 크게 웃기 시작했습니다! 그리고 우리는 옆구리를 움켜잡았어요! 그리고 우리는 땅바닥에서 이리저리 뒹굴었습니다!

"넌 괴짜야!" 잘생긴 워런이 말했습니다.

"너도 역시, 괴짜야!" 내가 대답했습니다.

"우리 둘 다 괴짜라고!" 그가 말했습니다.

그리고 그래서 그 후, 나와 괴짜 워런은 뒹굴며 웃고 또 뒹굴며 웃었습니다. 잔디밭 이곳저곳을요. 종이 칠 때까지 말이죠!

왜냐면 물론, 그게 바로 괴짜들이 하는 행동이니까요!

그리고 또 내 생각에, 나와 그는 새 친구가 된 것 같아요!

그리고 그것은 바로 그리고 행복하게 살았답니다라는 결말인 거죠!

Chapter 1

1. D Me and that Grace and Lucille play horses together before school. Horses is when you gallop. And trot. And snort. I am Brownie. Lucille is Blackie. And that Grace is Yellowie. Only today, me and that Grace couldn't find Lucille anywhere. We looked all over the place for her.

2. B "GO AWAY, BOY! GO AWAY AND LEAVE LUCILLE ALONE!" she shouted. "YES!" I yelled. "LEAVE LUCILLE ALONE! OR I WILL TELL PRINCIPAL ON YOU! 'CAUSE ME AND HIM ARE PERSONAL FRIENDS. AND HE WILL POUND YOUR HEAD!" After that, me and that Grace kept on shooing our arms until he ran away. Then we did a high five. "HURRAY!" we shouted. "HURRAY! HURRAY! WE SAVED LUCILLE FROM THE EVIL STRANGER BOY!"

3. C All of a sudden, Lucille came stomping at us very angry. "WHY DID YOU DO THAT?" she hollered. "WHY DID YOU CHASE THAT BOY AWAY? NOW YOU'VE RUINED EVERYTHING!" Me and that Grace looked surprised at her. "But we thought you wanted us to do that," said that Grace. "We saved you from the evil stranger boy," I explained very proud. Lucille did a mad breath. "He is not an evil stranger boy, Junie B.! He's a new kid in Room Eight. And his name is Warren! And he's the handsomest boy I ever saw! He's even been in a TV commercial before!"

4. D Then my eyes practically popped out of my head! 'Cause he was handsome like a movie star! That's why! "Wowie-wow-wow! What a chunk!" I said. "I would like him for my new boyfriend, I think!"

5. A "Yeah, only here's the problem, Lucille," I said. "Me and Grace didn't actually get a crack at him yet." "Yeah," said that Grace. "We definitely need a crack at him. And so now you have to introduce us." Lucille stamped her foot. "No!" she yelled. "No! No! No! 'Cause you guys will steal him away from me! And that's not even fair! Plus, Junie B. already has a boyfriend. Remember, Junie B.? You already have Ricardo! Remember?"

Chapter 2

1. C After that, I showed Lucille my socks, too. "See, Lucille? See mine? They are very sagging and droopy. That's because last night me and my dog Tickle played tug-of-war with those things. And he got drooly on them." Lucille made a face. "Eew," she said. "I know they are eew," I said back. "That's what I've been trying to tell you, Lucille. I am a big pig. And so how can I even steal your boyfriend?"

2. A "Now we are friends again! Right, Lucille? Right?" I said. "And so now you can introduce me to Handsome Warren. 'Cause I won't even steal that guy." Lucille fluffed herself some more. "I don't know . . . I'll think about it," she said. I clapped my hands real thrilled. Then I quick stood up on my chair. "GRACE! HEY, GRACE!" I hollered. "LUCILLE SAID SHE'LL THINK ABOUT IT!"

3. D Mrs. hurried up to my table. "Never ever stand up in your chair, Junie B.," she said. "You could fall off and break something."

4. B "Grace! Grace! Guess what? Lucille is going to introduce us to Handsome Warren! 'Cause you and me are big pigs, that's why!" That Grace looked upset at me. "I am not a big pig," she said. I quick whispered in her ear. "Yeah, only we're not really big pigs, Grace. We just have to say we're big pigs. Or else Lucille thinks we will steal her boyfriend. Get it?"

5. A I kept on laughing at that funny joke. Only too bad for me. 'Cause after while, I couldn't even stop. I was out of control, I think. I holded my sides and fell on the ground. Then I rolled and laughed and rolled and laughed. All around in the grass. Handsome Warren looked nervous of me. He backed up. "What a nutball," he said very soft.

Chapter 3

1. B That Grace crossed her arms, too. "I'm not stealing him away, Lucille. He just automatically loves me on his own. And there's nothing I can do about it," she said.

2. **D** She looked down at me. "Tell her, Junie B.! Tell Grace she can't steal my boyfriend!"

3. **A** And so I stood up from the grass. And I walked to Room Nine all by myself. 'Cause I couldn't stop thinking about being a nutball, that's why. I thought about it the whole rest of the day. I didn't even talk. Not at Show-and-Tell. Not at snacktime. Not even when I got on the bus to ride home.

4. **C** "I am not a nutball, Grace! I am just a regular normal girl. And I don't even know why that boy had to call me that!"

5. **C** "Yes," she said. "My two-year-old brother Jeffie is a nutball. Every time we go to the mall, we have to put him on a leash. Or else he tackles people. And then he hides in the clothes and Security has to come."

Chapter 4

1. **D** After that, my grandma let me pick a new cereal to eat. I picked a grown-up kind. It was the kind with fibers in it.

2. **C** All of a sudden, I clapped my hands very joyful. "Did you see me, Grace? Did you see how calm I was just then? That's because I don't have sugar in me today! And I can sit still very excellent!" I hugged her real tight. "It worked, Grace! The fiber cereal worked! Now I'm not a nutball anymore! And so Handsome Warren will love me just like he loves you!"

3. **A** And so just then, Handsome Warren and that Grace raced all over the playground. And he couldn't even beat her. He came back very pooped. "Wow," he said. "You're the fastest runner I ever saw. Maybe someday you'll be in the Olympics."

4. **D** "This dress costed over one hundred and fifty dollars . . . not including tax," she said. All of a sudden, Handsome Warren's eyes got big and wide. "Wow! You must be the richest girl in the whole school!" he said.

5. **B** "Hello. How are you today?" I said very pleasant. "I am fine. I am fine and calm." He backed up from me. "Yeah, only you don't even have to be afraid," I said. "'Cause I ate fibers for breakfast. And I am so calm I could go to

sleep, probably. Want to see me? Huh, Warren? Want to see me go to sleep?" I plopped down in the grass. "Look, Warren. See me down here? I am not even laughing and rolling. I am just being calm. And that's all."

Chapter 5

1. A "We gotta get to the mall! That's what's the hurry! We have to buy me a princess dress! Plus also I need some shoes with lightning!" Mother and Daddy looked funny at me. That's how come I had to explain all about Handsome Warren. And how he loved Lucille's princess dress. And how he loved Grace's fast shoes. "And so now I will get a princess dress! Plus also I will get shoes with lightning! And then Warren will love me, too!"

2. B "YOU GUYS DO THE DISHES!" I hollered to Mother and Daddy. "I'LL PUT OLLIE'S SWEATER ON HIS HEAD! 'CAUSE THAT WILL SAVE US TIME, I THINK!" I quick climbed into Ollie's crib. Then I tried to pull that baby's sweater on him. Only his giant head didn't fit through the hole.

3. D "Okay. I want you to listen to me. And I want you to listen carefully," she said. "You don't make friends by wearing new dresses or shoes with lightning. You make new friends by being fun to be with. And by being nice to people. And by caring about their feelings."

4. A "And honesty is important, too, Junie B.," she said. "You have to be honest with people. And that means that you can't pretend to be someone you're not." She smoothed my hair. "You're not Lucille, Junie B. And you're not Grace, either. You're just you. You're just Junie B. Jones. And believe me, that's a big enough job for anyone."

5. C "Look, Mother! Look what this bear is wearing! It is a ribbon made out of rich, red velvet! And that is 'zactly the kind of cloth I've been looking for!" I took the bow off the teddy. And I held it next to my hair. "How do I look? Huh, Mother? Do I look like a beautiful princess? Do I look gorgeous? Huh? Do I?"

Chapter 6

1. B "You sillyhead, Grace!" I said. "Don't you know anything? This is a lovely collar of jewels! It is the kind of jewels that princesses wear! Only I didn't even know we had this gorgeous thing! I found it where Mother keeps the dog food. Only I don't actually know why it got put there." I holded out my arms. "And did you notice these, Grace? Did you notice my long white princess gloves? They are the kind of gloves that Cinderella wears. And Cinderella is a real, actual princess. Plus also she does floors." I pointed at my head. "And what about this golden crown I am wearing? It is from a real actual Dairy Queen! Plus, also I have red velvet bows on my sneakers! And Mother even drew lightning on their sides. Just like yours!"

2. C Grace slumped down in her seat. She didn't talk the whole rest of the way to school.

3. A "Hello. How are you today? I am wearing princess clothes," I told him. Handsome Warren didn't look up.

4. B All of a sudden, Handsome Warren raised up his head. "GO AWAY!" he shouted. "ALL OF YOU! GO AWAY AND LEAVE ME ALONE!"

5. D Finally, Lucille did a huffy breath at him. "You're not being nice, Warren. You used to be nice. But now you're not. And so I don't even want to be your friend today." "Me, either," said that Grace. "I don't want to be your friend today, either!" Then both of those guys held hands. And they stomped away from there very furious.

Chapter 7

1. D "Guess what? There's something in your hair," I told him. I looked harder at that thing. "I think it's a teeny leaf. Or else maybe it's a piece of Kleenex," I said. He still didn't move. "Want me to brush it off for you?" I asked. "'Cause that would not be any trouble. And I would be happy to do it." I waited very patient for him to answer. Then I tapped on him some more.

2. A Handsome Warren did a grouchy face. "I'm not your friend," he said. "I

don't have any friends at this school. All my friends were at my other school. But then my dad made me move here. And now nothing is the same. I hate this place! I hate it! I hate it!"

3. C   After that, I sat very still. And I listened to Warren being sad. Finally I did a sigh. And I tried my very last idea. "Knock knock," I said.

4. B   Just then, Handsome Warren did a teeny smile. He waited for a second. Then he smiled some more. "Knock knock," he said. "Who's there?" "Icy," said Handsome Warren. "Icy who?" "Icy London, Icy France, Icy Lucille's underpants," he said.

5. B   Then me and Handsome Warren started laughing real hard! And we holded our sides! And we rolled all around on the ground! "YOU ARE A NUTBALL!" said Handsome Warren. "YOU ARE A NUTBALL, TOO!" I said back. "WE ARE BOTH NUTBALLS!" he said.

주니 B. 존스는 잘생긴 워런을 좋아해
(Junie B. Jones Loves Handsome Warren)

초판 발행   2022년 3월 4일

지은이   Barbara Park
편집   정소이 유아름
콘텐츠제작및감수   롱테일북스 편집부
번역   기나현
저작권   김보경
마케팅   김보미 정경훈

기획   김승규
펴낸이   이수영
펴낸곳   롱테일북스
출판등록   제2015-000191호
주소   04033 서울특별시 마포구 양화로 113(서교동) 3층
전자메일   helper@longtailbooks.co.kr
(학원·학교에서 본 도서를 교재로 사용하길 원하시는 경우 전자메일로 문의주시면
자세한 안내를 받으실 수 있습니다.)

ISBN 979-11-91343-14-4 14740